ORGANISATION FOR ECONOMIC CO-OPERATION AND DEVELOPMENT

ORGANISATION FOR ECONOMIC CO-OPERATION AND DEVELOPMENT

Pursuant to Article 1 of the Convention signed in Paris on 14th December 1960, and which came into force on 30th September 1961, the Organisation for Economic Co-operation and Development (OECD) shall promote policies designed:

- to achieve the highest sustainable economic growth and employment and a rising standard of living in Member countries, while maintaining financial stability, and thus to contribute to the development of the world economy;
- to contribute to sound economic expansion in Member as well as non-member countries in the process of economic development; and
- to contribute to the expansion of world trade on a multilateral, non-discriminatory basis in accordance with international obligations.

The original Member countries of the OECD are Austria, Belgium, Canada, Denmark, France, Germany, Greece, Iceland, Ireland, Italy, Luxembourg, the Netherlands, Norway, Portugal, Spain, Sweden, Switzerland, Turkey, the United Kingdom and the United States. The following countries became Members subsequently through accession at the dates indicated hereafter: Japan (28th April 1964), Finland (28th January 1969), Australia (7th June 1971), New Zealand (29th May 1973), Mexico (18th May 1994) and the Czech Republic (21st December 1995). The Commission of the European Communities takes part in the work of the OECD (Article 13 of the OECD Convention).

Publié en français sous le titre :

FORMULER DES MEILLEURES POLITIQUES POUR LE DÉVELOPPEMENT RURAL

FOREWORD

A High-Level Meeting of the Group of the Council on Rural Development was held in Paris at the OECD on April 10 and 11, 1995 in order to take stock of the continuing and increasing debate on rural issues in OECD countries. Issues include economic and social development as well as the role and coherence of rural policy in new territorial development strategies, and the role and impact of sectoral policies on rural development. This publication constitutes the follow-up of work carried out by the Rural Development Programme in 1993 establishing the framework of rural development policies in OECD countries (cf. *What Future for Our Countryside? A Rural Development Policy*, OECD, 1993).

Rural development policy has a territorial focus. It is concerned with thinly populated areas and small towns. These areas face major challenges posed by globalisation, increasing competitiveness, and the need to improve and safeguard environmental conditions. In certain areas, unemployment and a stagnating economy are the challenges ahead. In others, dealing with rapid growth in fast changing economic situations is the priority.

The High-Level Meeting placed particular emphasis on establishing programmes and strategies to promote locally-generated economic activities taking into account the diverse situations facing rural areas. High-ranking government officials used this meeting to discuss the reasons for the changes occurring in rural areas in OECD countries and how different governments were responding to the challenge. Moreover, they fully agreed on the importance to national economies of economically viable and environmentally healthy rural areas, both for the well being of rural inhabitants as well as other citizens.

This publication presents the papers given at the meeting by experts in the field and contributions from eight countries, as well as the main findings of the meeting. As such, it represents the current thinking by high-level policy makers on issues concerning rural development. Moreover, it gives concrete examples of how various member countries are designing and implementing policies to meet the new challenges faced by rural populations.

At the Ninth Session of the Group of the Council on Rural Development, in November 1995, it was recommended that in view of its interest, the proceedings from the High-Level Meeting should be derestricted. This report is published on the responsibility of the Secretary-General of the OECD.

TABLE OF CONTENTS

LIST OF TABLES AND FIGURES

MAIN FINDINGS OF THE HIGH-LEVEL MEETING OF THE GROUP OF THE COUNCIL ON RURAL DEVELOPMENT

Rural areas comprise 90 per cent of the land area and almost one third of the population of Member countries. For most countries rural areas represent a large share of the national economy and hence economically viable and environmentally healthy rural areas are an indispensable component of balanced national development. Rural areas must participate in national economic growth if the overall economy is to effectively exploit its potential, and the well-being for both rural inhabitants and other citizens is to be assured. This is the starting point for all further considerations of how to best shape rural development policies.

Rural development forms an important and integral part of policy agendas in OECD countries. Furthermore, the territorial focus of policies designed to encourage rural development has obliged policy makers in Member countries to rethink traditional sectoral based development strategies. With varying degrees of importance rural development policies in OECD Member countries have the following objectives:

- to enhance the competitiveness of rural areas so as to maximise their contribution to economic development;

- to provide opportunities for rural citizens to enjoy a standard of living comparable to national norms;

- to preserve and develop the natural environment and cultural heritage of rural areas.

New Perspectives and Strategies

The major forces bearing on rural areas are economic change, changing patterns of employment and new environmental demands. The globalisation of both production and demand, as well as the concurrent rapid changes in technologies, information flows and the composition of markets has

9

resulted in intensified competition. Most OECD countries benefit from this process. Some rural areas dominated by activities late in their respective product cycle, however, face difficult structural problems. In particular, problems related to structural changes in agriculture, as well as regional disparities, migration and unemployment resulting from industrial restructuring pose new and critical challenges. While some rural areas face difficult challenges, others have harnessed their economic potential resulting in employment creation rates which are above national averages.

Primary industries remain important in many rural areas, as they dominate land use in these areas. However, employment in manufacturing and services in rural areas greatly outnumbers employment in all primary industries combined. New ways must be found to support rural industries to help them to remain profitable and competitive, contributing to the economic growth of the area, as well as providing jobs. Mechanisms which nourish the existing dynamism in rural economies need to be put into place, to insure that these areas remain dynamic. One means of confronting the challenges posed by an ever increasingly globalisation of markets is through the creation of a well-educated and flexible labour force in rural areas.

Lastly, there is a growing importance of environmental concerns for rural areas. Rural areas do not always capture the fair return from society's use of their environmental, cultural and historical resources. Additionally, the demand for these resources is increasing with growing income levels. The contribution stemming from the appropriate *mise en valeur* of rural amenities to national wealth can be considerable. However, the trade-offs rural area face between economic development and environment preservation are difficult to resolve, and require close attention by both the public and private sector. Better mechanisms for resolving conflicts between national and local level government on these issues needs to be gradually implemented, including both market and non-market solutions.

It is important to underline that all of the present challenges facing rural areas and policy makers need to be viewed within a general context of ever decreasing financial resources for public policies and programmes. As a result, policy makers are presently shifting their focus to develop more effective ways of facilitating economic development by providing opportunities and appropriate economic climates rather than relying solely on direct financial transfers to spur growth in rural areas.

Given the diverse challenges facing rural areas, the OECD High-Level Meeting concentrated on two interrelated development issues central to economic growth in rural areas. These are employment creation and the establishment of a strong economic base for rural zones.

In a rapidly evolving global economy many of the traditional economic opportunities in rural areas are disappearing or changing in terms of the skills they require. Global integration also introduces new opportunities for rural areas. The seizing of economic opportunities presented by this changing economic landscape is thus central to the development policy of rural communities. National employment policies need to address the wide range of solutions and problems found in rural areas. Specifically, national employment policies must take into account the diverse situations in rural areas in terms of the labour force, labour markets, and the enterprise culture. Employment policies must capitalise on the private/public sector interface, with public sector policies stimulating the private sector and nurturing the entrepreneurial spirit found in rural areas.

Enhancing employment opportunities requires a creative strategy to stimulate entrepreneurship for new firms, new products, new markets and better business practices. Small indigenous firms have replaced subsidised branch plants as the most likely source of new employment in rural areas, due to reasons of effectiveness and tight budgets. Hence, increasing the number of entrepreneurs and improving the business climate will be critical factors in generating employment opportunities.

In order to capture the new opportunities created by changes in world trade patterns and constant technological innovation a new outlook on strategies for establishing a strong economic base in rural areas is required. Encouraging specialisation on a local level, while at the same time diversifying regionally appears to be the most constructive approach for rural areas. To that end, investment must be made in new means for rural places to become or remain competitive, such as a better skilled workforce, new forms of organisation of production, the exploitation of niche markets and the development of new mechanisms for co-operation between private sector agents.

Strategic Public Policies

Public policies play a crucial role in facilitating the transition required by the new global context. The OECD High-Level Meeting on rural development underscored the point that each country must develop its own

11

public policies for rural zones. The policy measures will not only reflect the peculiarities of each country but should also take into account the diversity found rural areas. These policies should concentrate on both short-term and long term development options from an economic, social, environmental perspective.

The meeting emphasised that the use of internationally comparable indicators provides a sound basis for analysis and decision-making, helping governments and rural populations seize the full range of opportunities presented in rural areas. Significant progress in identifying some important elements of public policy for rural development was made at the meeting and are summarised below.

Partnerships

Ensuring co-ordination between different levels of government is critical in the development process of rural zones. Central government supports both regional and local leadership thereby playing a key role in this process. But the way this support is implemented is critical to the effectiveness of the policy measures carried out at the various levels of government. In a system where innovation is encouraged at lower levels, the issue is not that of policy measures *per se*, but of different actors working independently towards common goals. With this perspective, the way in which strategic options are decided and the partnerships for implementing them are critical. Increasingly, successful and innovative partnerships among the public, private and voluntary sectors will be a key to the integration of rural economies in the global market place.

Sectoral Policies with a Territorial Approach

Sectoral policies reflect the way in which most countries organise government and implement policy. This is a handicap for rural areas as national sectoral policies are often implemented without taking into account the regional or local context. Sectoral policies based on a territorial diagnosis should create a more appropriate mix of policies for rural areas and contribute to the formulation of horizontal, multi-sectoral and collaborative policy strategies. Sectoral policies need to have a rural development dimension built into them. Furthermore, a better understanding of the role or impact of sectoral policies on the development process would facilitate effective complementarity of sectoral policies aimed at rural development within Member countries.

Agriculture and Rural Development

The economic character of rural areas is no longer synonymous with agriculture. Although agriculture employs a large portion of the rural population in some OECD countries, the overall employment significance of agriculture is relatively modest, and will most likely decline in the future. At the same time, agriculture continues to play a defining role in rural landscapes and is a vector of great public support for rural areas. Given these facts, it is essential to recognise agriculture as one component to be incorporated into a comprehensive rural development strategy.

Economic Diversity in Rural Areas

Strategies to stimulate and encourage economic development in rural areas must recognise that there is growing sectoral diversification in many rural areas. Employment creation trends illustrate this fact. In many member countries the share of industrial employment is higher for rural regions than for urban regions. Moreover, in many rural areas the service sector provides one job in two. The newly emerging pattern of sectoral structures in rural areas means that government policies must be sensitive to these trends. Policy mechanisms should encourage growth in newly established sectors through a variety a tools, including the stimulation of private sector initiatives.

Labour Markets

Active labour market policies that incorporate sufficient flexibility to deal with rural conditions are vital for improving employment opportunities. Distance and low density make many current employment policies of limited value to many rural areas. At the same time, the need for improved education and training is particularly critical in rural places. Such measures must be closely linked to business creation and expansion policies.

Information Technology

The availability of new information technology and the emergence of information highways will critically influence the future of rural areas. They offer the promise of alleviating the disadvantages that come with distance and low density. But, successful adaptation is not assured. Failure to ensure that rural areas are adequately linked to the new information infrastructure will make many forms of development impossible.

Governance

There is a need for improving rural governance in order to facilitate the economic and social development of rural communities. New methods continue to be needed to build bridges between top down policies and bottom up initiatives. Because rural areas differ so widely in their opportunities and problems, the current government policy trend of devolving responsibility to local areas is important. Devolution has the potential to increase local leadership and responsibility for rural development policy. Central governments, however, continue to play a key role as they alone have the capacity to compensate for the most extreme disparities in resources among rural communities. It is important to note that prior to the implementation of any activities it is critical to set strategic goals and priorities. Additionally, rural development policies must take into account the constraint of tight budgets and the need to make strategic investments that support local initiative in the economic, social and environmental fields.

Priorities

Rural areas face and will continue to face many challenges in their attempts to integrate into the global economy. Continuing monitoring and analysis of the changes affecting many rural areas as a result of globalisation of the economy and structural change involving the main rural industries remains a priority. In practical terms, more work should be carried out on creating employment opportunities, developing business in rural areas, and on realising the potential of the cultural and environmental heritage of these areas.

PART I   RURAL DEVELOPMENT IN AN EVOLVING CONTEXT

CHAPTER 1   OPENING STATEMENT,
MR. JEAN-CLAUDE PAYE, SECRETARY-GENERAL, OECD

It is an honour for me to welcome you to the first High-Level Meeting on Rural Development.

Nearly eight years ago, the OECD Council at Ministerial level included the question of rural development on the Organisation's work agenda for the first time. It is timely that senior policy makers in this area should meet today to review what has been done and discuss how to approach the challenges facing our societies in this connection.

The growing interdependence of the world economy and changing systems of production and trade, while opening broad prospects of progress, are giving rise to tensions in our societies which can endanger the harmonious development of many parts of our countries.

Globalisation and balanced development of national territories

The striking feature of Globalisation is that it introduces a continuous process of adjustment into our societies. But that process does not take place uniformly throughout the national territory. Globalisation does not automatically generate the same economic, social and environmental benefits everywhere, nor do they necessarily occur simultaneously. It is therefore the responsibility of governments to ensure that the capacity to adjust of all types of territory, whether rural or urban, is strengthened.

The stakes are considerable. The issue is not simply one of economic equity designed to enable all citizens to benefit from growth, regardless of where they live and work. The issue is also of major political importance since the harmonious development of the entire national territory is a basic pre-condition for the social cohesion of a country and, consequently, for its political stability.

This continuous process of adaptation will be able to occur more rapidly if those concerned have the means to take the necessary and most relevant decisions. To this end most of our Member countries have taken steps to decentralise government responsibility in areas such as labour markets, local economic development policies, infrastructure investment and so on. In other fields, central government policies are increasingly drawn up in close collaboration with regional and local levels and, in many cases, in partnership with the private sector.

Issues and disadvantages of rural areas

The Rural Development Programme acquires its full significance against this background of globalisation and the search for balanced development of our territories.

Globalisation is placing certain rural areas in a very difficult situation, requiring particularly far-reaching adjustment on their part. The use of new technologies in fisheries, forestry and above all agriculture, has led to the disappearance of a large number of jobs in rural areas. Manufacturing industries and other secondary activities, which people in rural areas saw a source of new jobs, have in their turn experienced an overall decline. What is more, the countryside still lags somewhat in the development of service activities, particularly as regards producer services. These factors have led to large-scale movements of labour, particularly towards the towns.

But this vision of the countryside does not means that the problems are really fundamental ones. Very few rural areas in the OECD countries are in a critical situation when looked at in terms of world-wide criteria. And most have an extremely solid human and natural resource base. This base comprises not only a potential for agriculture and for leisure, but also the capacity to offer a style of living and working which is more agreeable and more human than that often found in the cities. The relocation of enterprises to rural areas clearly shows that the latter do have recognised competitive advantages. Furthermore, the services sector, which is able to benefit directly from the possibilities of information technologies, seems extremely promising. Lastly, all countries have rural landscapes where innovative policies regarding infrastructure, communications and the spreading of holidays throughout the year, can be exploited in a sustainable way.

Rural development is above all a question of multi-sectoral policy requiring close co-operation between the various authorities concerned. Consequently, several Committees of the Organisation have examined the impact of their own policy on rural development. A document setting out the results obtained through this horizontal co-operation has been provided and I can assure you that the Council continues to give priority to such horizontal activities.

Orientation of the Rural Development Programme

The mandate of the Group of the Council on Rural Development will be submitted to the Council of the OECD in the coming weeks. Your meeting therefore offers an opportunity to consider the possible orientations of this Programme. In this context, I should like to mention certain elements that seem to me of particular importance.

– The first obviously concerns employment. I should like here to stress that while unemployment is severely affecting our societies as a whole, it hits rural society in an even more drastic manner. Diversification of activities in rural areas seems the only solution to the problem of how to create jobs and enterprises. Favourable conditions for strengthening the economic fabric therefore have to be put in place;

– secondly, rural areas have specific advantages. Each of them has its specific economic and social, but also cultural and environmental attributes. Given this, thought has been given to how best to exploit them. Examples of success are numerous in our countries and there is an urgent need to exchange experience in this field;

– thirdly, there is the role and impact of sectoral policies. The effectiveness and complementarity of sectoral policies are manifest in territorial, and more particularly rural terms. The impact of sectoral policies on rural areas must be kept under review, particularly since rural economies are relatively fragile and mistakes in policy can be more costly than elsewhere;

– lastly, rural development is still imperfectly understood. Or rather our understanding does not measure up to what is at stake in economic and political terms. It is therefore vital to make the results of the current work better known and to reflect on how to continue our action in this area.

Eight years after the Council of the OECD asked the Organisation to undertake work on rural development, there are no longer disputes over the importance of a subject which directly concerns a third of the OECD population and covers nine-tenths of its territory. It is clear that our governments now realise that this is a key policy issue in the harmonious development of our national territories. Your presence at this meeting today is the proof of that and I am certain that your discussions will contribute to the improved design of rural development policies.

CHAPTER 2   STATEMENT BY MR. KENNETH L. DEAVERS, CHAIRMAN OF THE GROUP OF THE COUNCIL ON RURAL DEVELOPMENT FROM 1990 TO 1994

Introduction

I attended the first meeting that the OECD held to discuss rural development in 1981. Coming as it did at the end of a decade or "rural Renaissance" in many Member countries, it was infused with hope for a new prosperity, as rural areas benefited from strong trends of rural population growth, increasing employment, and rising incomes. Balanced economic development, which Member countries sought, seemed to be attainable. Organised by the OECD Secretariat of the Technical Co-operation Committee (TECO), much of the 1981 meeting focused on institutional changes designed to enhance the underlying trend toward a prosperous and vital future for rural citizens of Member countries.

Nearly fifteen years later, looking back at our discussions, it is easy to be critical about the naive optimism that we shared. The intervening years have been a period of significant economic upheaval throughout the developed economies, with many rural areas left at the margin of economic progress enjoyed by other members of the society. Changes in technology, capital mobility and information flows, consumer tastes and markets, production and distribution systems, emerging environmental concerns and constraints, and other factors -- all occurring at an unprecedented pace -- have seriously tested the ability of governments to respond with effective policies and programmes for balanced development.

It took some time for economists to realise how profound the changes in rural spatial advantage and disadvantage were, and for the OECD to mount a serious effort to deal with the need for a coherent knowledge base from which to advise Member countries about how their policy approaches and institutional arrangements might be made more effective in fostering rural development. In organising the Rural Development Programme (RDP) as a Group of the Council in July 1990, the OECD formally recognised the role of territory, or more precisely economic space, in mediating the operation of markets and distributing the benefits of economic progress. The launching of the new Territorial Development Service last July 1994 was another important step in the process.

I want to examine some of the lessons from the work of the Rural Development Programme -- which should be understood to include the active support and work of the delegates represented on the Group of the Council, as well as that of the Secretariat. I believe the lessons have importance for Member countries as they seek to assure a balance of societal benefits that come from national economic development. They are also significant to the future work of the Territorial Development Service. I want to end by looking at some of the future challenges facing rural areas in Member countries, and their implications for the Rural Development Programme.

Lessons from the Rural Development Programme

Three principles have guided the work of the Secretariat and Group of the Council from their inception. They are:

- the substantive work on rural development must be based on a solid conceptual framework, reflecting national interests in rural territory and people, and informed by a general understanding of the major trends that give the issue political salience in Member countries;

- there must be an empirical framework to measure what is happening in the rural territory of Member countries, based on a consistent and agreed territorial delineation. Measurement, after all, is a major currency of the OECD because it makes better informed discussion and debate possible. Among Member countries whose rural territory is very diverse, the absence of meaningful measurement reduces international discussions to exchanges of non-comparable case studies and anecdotes. These are seldom a sound basis for policy advice;

– specific work undertaken by the Secretariat should be focused on important policy questions identified by the Member countries. Because of its unique international role, the OECD can link these national policy questions to key challenges that occur across many economic sectors and countries. The purpose of the OECD work is to assist national policy makers in the difficult task of improving rural development policies and programmes. The work should be rigorous in its analytical approach, but not academic in its conclusions.

Agreement on a territorial grid, which made possible the collection of preliminary indicators describing rural areas of Member countries, illustrates clearly why rural issues matter. Overall, in the OECD Member countries, nearly one third of the population lives in rural areas, and more than 90 per cent of national territory is rural space. But these data also lead to important insights. One is the tremendous diversity *within* rural areas of Member countries as well as between them. This points up how difficult the task of articulating effective rural development policies is for national authorities; one size fits all rural policies are doomed to fail. Similarly, it makes untenable the assumption that if national authorities simply get their macro and sectoral policies right, space does not matter.

The Rural Development Programme has to respond to public policy questions that do not neatly fall under the authority of any particular ministry. Within the Rural Development Programme, and now for TDS, a key question is how to advise Member countries on the formulation and implementation of territorial policies that must be horizontal, multi-sectoral, and collaborative, while government policies remain largely vertical, sectoral, and hierarchical.

The structure of our governments is not likely to change fundamentally. Yet, if rural development policies are to be effectively conceived and implemented, a diverse group of ministries must be involved, governments at all levels will have a role to play, and the private sector must be made a full partner. The Group of the Council has clearly demonstrated the value of participation from many ministries in OECD deliberations on rural development policy. And the Secretariat's recently held workshop on niche markets is an excellent example of how representatives from subsidiary levels of government, non-governmental organisations, and the private sector can enrich policy discussion and analysis, and enhance the relevance of policy advice.

The task of the Rural Development Programme in the OECD has been made more complicated by the accepted wisdom about the economic character of rural areas; that rural and agriculture are synonymous. Indicator data collected for Member countries makes clear how dysfunctional a single sectoral definition of rural areas is. For RDP, the Agriculture Directorate, and the OECD, I believe that debate is now settled. But the solution did not come easily, and nor is it as widely understood outside the OECD as it is within. Some interests within agriculture want to subsume rural development policy within agriculture policy, in part to enhance the importance of their sphere of responsibility. At the same time, some rural policy advocates want to deny agriculture policy any role whatsoever. There are serious risks in both extremes.

Data on the economic structure of rural territory, compiled as part of the Group of the Council's work, show that agriculture employs a significant share of rural people in many areas of Member countries. However, the overall employment significance of agriculture is modest, and as the OECD itself has said, it almost certainly will decline for most Member countries in the future. Because of this, dependence on agriculture as the principal source of employment is typically a difficult challenge for rural areas as they seek future development opportunities. Yet, agriculture plays a major role in shaping the rural landscape, and it remains a well-spring of national support for "rural development". Given these facts, it seems useful to recognise agriculture as one component of horizontality that must be encompassed in a comprehensive rural development policy. Viewing agriculture in this way is likely to lead to different policies than those of the recent past; policies that could significantly enhance the achievement of societal goals for rural development.

A review of the lessons of the RDP would be incomplete if it did not recognise the many dimensions of development that countries want their rural policies to accomplish. Within the OECD, it should come as no surprise that employment and income are critically important. No rural development policy scheme can succeed if it fails to focus on the creation of opportunities for rural people to engage in rewarding, private, market-driven employment and enterprises. The *sine qua non* of the last decade of the 20th century, with the collapse of the planned economy model, is government as a facilitator and catalyst - not the creator of wealth and development opportunities.

Member countries also want rural areas to play a role in the overall quality of life experienced by all citizens. Because so much of the national territory is rural -- landscape, life-styles and indigenous cultures, unique products, monuments, and history -- it is critical in shaping national identity. Pioneering theoretical work undertaken by the RDP on *rural amenities* has set the stage for future policy work that can move us from romantic expressions of the rural idyll, to practical ways of facilitating its achievement. These policies should not be viewed as largely transfer or welfare programmes for rural people.

Indeed, if they are appropriately chosen and carefully administered they can make a net positive contribution to national wealth and income. Like GDP accounts and environmental balance sheets, they should be measured and monitored for their contribution to national well-being. This requires that we recognise and measure as best as we can their *mise en valeur*, and develop appropriate policies to assure that amenities contribute fully to rural development.

Challenges facing the Rural Development Programme

The first challenge facing RDP (in fact, the entire newly established TDS) is to find a way of framing rural development issues and its policy analyses to connect more directly with the OECD's major preoccupation of employment creation. There are many sceptics within the OECD that territory matters in economic development, or if it does matter, whether it is an important concern for national policy makers. What is clear to me is that employment policy advice coming from the OECD to Member countries will be seriously flawed if these sceptics prevail. While the specific institutional arrangements differ, based on history and culture, *all* Member countries organise their governments around units of geography: state or region, village or town, precinct or prefecture, county or canton. The work of the RDP clearly demonstrates that uniform national economic policies often have dramatically different effects across these units of political geography. If these differences consistently disadvantage rural citizens and territory, it will seriously test social cohesion and national governance. Moreover, national economic performance will be jeopardised.

The multidimensional concept of development encompassed in RDP must be retained. There are two risks. The first is that rural development will be seen as a trade-off between efficiency and equity. Rural development as defined by RDP is a societal goal, but it is not a social (transfer) programme. Rural people, who fall below social norms of well-being established by individual countries, may well be the targets of policies and programmes to improve their lot. But that is because they are citizens of the nation state -- partners in the social contract. *It is not because they are rural.* However, the specific social policies and programmes, and their implementation strategies, may be quite different as between rural and urban residents.

The second risk is that government's efforts to promote efficient, market-oriented rural development will fail to recognise and account for uniquely rural assets -- landscape, culture, history, etc. -- that contribute to national life and societal well-being. The *mise en valeur* of these assets must be recognised in establishing and evaluating rural development policy goals. The RDP work on public amenities is in its early stages, and establishing a rigorous framework to proceed has been technical and academic. However, I believe the future direction of the work holds great promise for practical policy advice on how to promote "sustainable development". Some policy makers express concern that past policies needing to be changed or abandoned will find new life under this tent. That could happen, but it is not an inevitable outcome. Moreover, the greater danger is that national economic development policy will fail to take advantage of market opportunities, public amenities and societal interest in a majority of the territory of the nation; and fail to deal explicitly with the economic consequences of sparse, remote, and low-density settlement. If that happens, national economic development will fall below its potential.

One of the important tasks for the RDP has been to encourage a horizontal policy perspective within the OECD. The idea, as expressed by the Group of the Council, is to plant the "rural gene" throughout the work of the organisation. RDP has been effective in doing this with several directorates and committees: agriculture, tourism, environment and statistics for example. And the country studies in Finland and Switzerland illustrate how important this work can be to Member countries which are in the process of assessing their future rural development policies and implementation strategies. This is time consuming work that is often invisible when taking stock of the "product" of the RDP, but it is critically important that it continue as a key element of the Secretariat's mandate. A related point is that most of the horizontal linkages for RDP are to directorates and committees outside of TDS -- horizontality in this sense is about the multi-sectoral policies that comprise comprehensive rural development.

The work on rural indicators needs to proceed by expanding and upgrading the statistics and information data base to more fully reflect the many dimensions of rural development of significance to Member countries. The indicators are important because they give substance and concreteness to the conceptual framework that underpins the work of the RDP. They help to identify specific rural case studies which can provide policy makers with an explanation of the relative effectiveness of various policy instruments, institutional arrangements, and implementation strategies. They also provide a basis for periodic assessment and reports of the status of rural areas and people across the OECD. No other organisation is in a position to carry out this work within an agreed international territorial framework. In many cases, work by the

OECD on measurement of rural development concepts encourages other international organisations and national authorities to improve their own measures and underlying data sources.

Conclusion

(...) It is clear that to accomplish their overall goals for economic improvement and broader societal well-being, OECD Member countries must have prosperous and vital rural areas. The RDP has begun to suggest ways in which governments policies can contribute to crating a future for rural citizens and the countryside. Thus, every country represented in the OECD has a stake in the success of the work undertaken by RDP.

CHAPTER 3   STATEMENT BY MADAME GUNHILD ØYANGEN, CHAIRMAN OF THE HIGH-LEVEL MEETING

The first High-Level Meeting devoted to rural development policy questions in Member countries was held on 10-11 April 1995. The meeting was chaired by Ms. Gunhild Øyangen, Norwegian Minister of Agriculture, and was opened by Mr. Jean-Claude Paye, Secretary-General of the OECD.

During the meeting top policy officials of the 25 Member countries exchanged points of view notably on the following questions: *(i)* employment in rural areas, *(ii)* diversification and specialisation of economic activities in rural areas, *(iii)* the role of different partners in rural development strategies, and *(iv)* co-ordination of sectoral policies. The delegates also drew lessons from past work by OECD. On this basis they provided guidelines concerning future work.

The delegations expressed overwhelming support for an extension of the mandate of the Rural Development Programme. Past work was seen as having contributed in a very positive way to the rural policy of Member countries. Several interventions recognised the strategic importance of territorial research to the other parts of the OECD, particularly the ongoing work on employment. The horizontal work of the secretariat was seen as particularly important. A number of delegations raised concerns with the limited resources available to the Rural Programme and suggested that the Council should seriously consider committing more resources to this vital programme.

Background

Over the next decade rural areas will need to make critical adjustments in their economies and society resulting particularly from our more open global production and trading systems, and the introduction of new technologies. This requires new approaches to public policy which are both more responsive to the specificities of place, and also capable of working with the private sector and encouraging entrepreneurship for new firms, products, and services. In this context, rural areas can become better places to live, and create more opportunities for income and employment which can help to stabilise populations. This will require changes in many existing policies.

Rural areas comprise 90 per cent of the land area and almost one third of the population of our Member countries. They provide virtually all our primary resources and much of our environmental, and cultural heritage. Rural areas are highly diverse, exhibiting wide ranges in average *per capita* income, having a variety of economic bases, and different degrees of attachment to the national and global economies. They are of value to all our citizens, both rural and urban.

Primary industries remain important in many rural areas, in particular because they are the dominant user of land. However, rural employment in manufacturing is higher than employment in all the primary industries combined. Currently rural industries face an uncertain future and therefore new ways to organise rural industries must be found so that they can remain profitable and continue to generate wealth and jobs.

In too many places unemployment and underemployment are high, household incomes are low, and access to basic services is inadequate. Disparities between different parts of the territory lead to a loss of national cohesion. Therefore public policy must take into account the need to maintain territorial integrity, for economic and social reasons. This requires that the broader social environment encourages a well educated and flexible labour force.

In the past, governments sought to overcome the disadvantages of distance and low density through transfer payments or through regulatory measures that compelled business to provide uniform levels of service. These methods have been costly for both government and private business and seem less promising for the future than measures seeking to create the conditions necessary for widening and building an indigenous economic base, improving the skills of rural residents and stimulating entrepreneurship.

Critical Rural Issues

The main goal for rural areas is to achieve sustainable rural development that can adapt to ongoing economic, environmental and social change. To achieve the goal will require co-operative actions within communities by business, local organisations and various levels of government.

New co-ordinated investments from public and private sources will be required to improve human capital, modernise industry and upgrade the infrastructure of rural areas.

Successfully confronting the challenges facing rural areas means taking the spatial dimension into account. Distance and low density are characteristic features of rural areas. Distance is commonly measured in a spatial sense, but it also includes remoteness in terms of access to information and to markets. Low density is a related feature. Because people are dispersed, it is more costly for them to communicate and interact. Some rural areas are already taking advantage of new opportunities, and in these places economic opportunities and income levels are expanding.

OECD data show that non-agricultural employment growth in some rural areas has been well in excess of national averages; other areas remain well behind national trends. The fact that some rural regions are increasing employment and creating a new economic base demonstrates that it is possible to make the transition successfully. Rural areas contribute to our societies in another important way. They are home to a wide range of natural and man-made features -- also called amenities that have both use and existence value. While certain amenities offer new opportunities for improving income and employment, others have value not because they can be marketed, but because they are an important part of the national and cultural heritage.

Expanding the Opportunity to Produce

Enhancing employment opportunities requires a more creative development strategy which stimulates entrepreneurship for new firms, new products, new markets and better business. In rural areas, increasing the number of entrepreneurs and improving the business climate will be critical factors in generating employment opportunities. Small indigenous firms have replaced subsidised branch plants as the most likely source of new employment in rural areas, due to reasons of effectiveness and tight budgets.

Rural areas will also have to find ways to bring employment opportunities to those who in the past have been less active in the labour market. This will require improving education and skills and linking these to market opportunities. In particular, women in rural areas suffer from a lack of suitable job possibilities. Planning of rural services will also need to take account of gender questions, men and women work and live in different ways and with different constraints; thus particular attention will be required to maximise the avenues open to women entrepreneurs and business creators.

Globalisation, new technology and the reorganisation of government are all affecting rural industries. Primary industries, such as agriculture, are providing even less employment as they adapt to global competition and to reduced levels of government subsidy. Yet, in certain rural areas primary industries remain the main source of income and employment. This requires us to improve the linkages between these basic sectors and examine possibilities for their expansion and growth. The entrepreneurial skills of the farm population can also provide a potential base for expanding the business base of rural regions. The same structural pressures also affect most manufacturing industries in rural areas. Increasing levels of competition threaten the future of many branch plants established in rural areas. The private sector in rural manufacturing industries must invest in new ways to remain competitive, such as better skilled workforces, new forms of organisation of production, and the development of specialisation through encouraging new systems of co-operation between themselves and opening up niche markets.

Enhancing Rural Amenities

Environmental improvement can provide new possibilities for economic and employment activity. Rural areas contain most of our natural resources, and a number of our built and cultural assets. There is an increasing demand for these amenities. Enhancing the environment and developing it successfully is likely to require further limits on uses, e.g. restricting clear cutting or strip mining activities, that create an undesirable environment. But, part of the resulting loss of revenue can be offset by increased income from new amenity based activities. In other cases, activities that preserve environmental quality need to be encouraged. To the extent that rural amenities have social value in excess of the price the market sets, there may be an argument for new public policy. More effective internalisation of both positive and negative externalities can improve the competitive position of rural areas. This will ensure that the full spectrum of services that the environment, broadly defined, provides is recognised. Amenities are of critical importance for the future of rural areas and should have a prominent place in the future work of the OECD Rural Development Programme.

The Role of Public Policies

Creating dynamic rural economies provides the best opportunity to address the gaps between standards of living between much of the rural territory of the OECD countries and urban areas. A high incidence of poverty and limited economic opportunity in rural areas creates major social and economic problems for our countries that will only get worse as the forces of change increase in pressure. They will also add to internal migration pressure and further strain our urban systems. While we do not yet have a complete strategy to shape new public policies we have made significant progress in identifying some important elements and establishing priorities for the future.

Because rural areas differ so widely in their opportunities and problems, the current trend of government policy that is devolving responsibility to local areas is important. Devolution has the potential advantage of increasing local ownership and responsibility for rural development policy. It is important that this process be accompanied by appropriate government support that is co-ordinated with local initiatives.

Active labour market policies that incorporate sufficient flexibility to deal with rural conditions are vital for improving employment opportunities. Distance and low density make many current employment policies of limited value to many rural areas. At the same time, the need for improved education and training is particularly critical in rural places. Such measures must be closely linked to business creation and expansion policies.

A number of sectoral policies have a major impact on rural areas. The OECD has already started to examine the contribution of the agricultural sector to rural development. It is now urgent to examine the impact of other sectorial policies, in particular environmental policy. Such studies would facilitate a better understanding of how to better manage the co-ordination of sectorial policies within Member countries.

The availability of new information technology and the emergence of information highways will critically influence the future of rural areas. They offer the promise of alleviating the disadvantages that come with distance and low density. But, successful adaptation is not assured. Failure to ensure that rural areas are adequately linked to the new information infrastructure will make many forms of development impossible. It appears unlikely that adequate investment in information technology and in the training to use it, will take place in rural areas without public support.

A significant task Member countries have to undertake is the collection and dissemination of territorially disaggregated statistics that help develop strategies for rural development. Some difficulties confronted are partly attributed to the lack of region- and community-specific information. Rural indicators clearly show the extent to which conditions differ among rural places.

Public policies play a crucial role in facilitating the transition to the global economy. Rural areas can make important contributions to our Member countries, but there is a pressing need for a new system of rural governance that can facilitate the economic and social development of rural communities. New methods are needed to build bridges between top down policies and bottom up initiatives. Before any partnership activities are implemented it is critical to set strategic goals and priorities. Rural development policies must take into account the constraint of tight budgets and the need to make strategic investments that support local initiative in the economic, social and environmental fields. To be effective, policies have to be tailored to the specific features of particular places and be sufficiently flexible to deal with the diversity of rural places.

PART II   COUNTRY CONTRIBUTIONS

UK Gov concern: Rural areas should be places where people live and work and the countryside should fully contribute to the national economy

(1) - How many people living in Rural England, Rise in rural accessible areas
    - Long term decline in employment in traditional industries "au profit de" tourism, manufacturing

(2) ↳ Need to improve number and quality of job opportunities in order to diversify local economies
    ↳ Restore the age profile in rural areas

(1) because of improved transport and telecom, older people with some spare money increasing demand for goods and services while younger people are out-migrating in search of jobs, better education and housing

3 Key Objectives for Policy
1- Invest in technology for an efficient food production
2- Spare areas for conservation
3- Invest in eco-tourism
   (nurturing an entrepreneurial climate)

CHAPTER 4   JOBS AND SKILLS FOR RURAL DEVELOPMENT

United Kingdom

Introduction

This paper addresses the *English* rural experience. The lessons from English rural development are not directly comparable with those from Scotland, Wales and Northern Ireland. The English countryside faces significantly greater pressure from competing demands on land use and from population growth. There are over 10 million people living and working in rural England. The Rural Development Commission (RDC) targets most of its direct financial assistance on 31 Rural Development Areas (RDAs), which encompass about one third of the rural population and where there is a concentration of economic and social problems. The RDAs cover the relatively more remote parts of England, but they probably would not be classified as remote in absolute terms or by comparison with some regions in other OECD Member countries.

In common with all OECD countries, the overall picture in the rural economy is one of long-term decline in employment in traditional industries together with the more recent downturn in jobs related to defence, which has been an important sector in rural England for the past fifty years. This is coupled with counter-balancing rises in rural employment in services, including tourism (although traditional seaside tourism continues to decline in many areas), and in manufacturing, and with a continuing rise in the rural population, particularly in the more accessible areas. In areas accessible to major towns there is a significant element of commuting to urban workplaces by car and by train.

The policy of the Rural Development Commission, endorsed by the UK government, is that English rural areas should be places where people both live and work, and that the countryside should make a full contribution to the national economy. In rural England local people of limited means can find it difficult to secure affordable housing and permanent jobs and have reasonable access to a range of good quality services. This is partly because of the in-migration of wealthier, better-qualified people from urban areas and partly because of the decline of traditional areas of employment. Policy responses are complicated by the lack of homogeneity among English rural areas and there is a broad division between the stronger economies of more accessible areas and the more land-based economies of remote districts. However, in most rural areas there is a need to improve the number and quality of job opportunities and, in the more remote areas, to continue to diversify local economies. In England the main policy aim is to help create the conditions in which rural communities can survive and prosper. It is very much a question of enabling local people and local businesses to create jobs in rural areas and for employment needs to be provided for locally. This is done mainly through the application of national programmes aimed at unemployment, training and enterprise support, supplemented in the more remote areas by relatively small and highly targeted rural development programmes (RDPs) promoted by the RDC, together with the deployment of RDC business advisory services targeted on rural small firms in those areas.

The changing employment structure of rural areas: convergence

In 1950 there were around a million people working on the land in England, but by 1994 this had fallen to just over 400 000. Extractive industries have also declined considerably from their former position as a major employer in rural areas. There are now only 5 500 people employed in coal mines in rural areas, compared to over 60 000 ten years ago and employment in quarrying has fallen by over 30 per cent in the same period.

Evidence suggests, however, that local rural economies, particularly in the more accessible areas, have generally adapted to the decline in employment in traditional industries. The basis for the rise of manufacturing and service activities in rural areas has been the development of new technologies since the Second World War, which do not require traditional industrial and commercial locations, and a movement of population from the cities into the nearer countryside. This is particularly true since the 1960s.

There has thus been a convergence of the employment profile and industrial structure of rural and urban areas. Most rural jobs are in services and manufacturing. However, the more remote rural areas retain a stronger land-based element and are probably not dynamic enough economically to adjust fully to the continuing changes in the national industrial structure and the increased level of competition.

While there are examples of strong local economies in the more accessible areas, earnings are lower on average in rural areas and, because of in-migration and restrictions on new development, housing costs can be higher than average. There is also emerging a mismatch between those skills for jobs in the declining industries in rural areas and those for the jobs that are replacing them. The declining provision of some services is also of importance as local services help facilitate a robust local economy and employment opportunities. The lack of convenient public transport services is a constraining factor on the location of jobs and on those looking for work, as well as causing more general problems for those without access to private transportation.

mismatch
commuting

Population

Rural life-style aspirations, coupled with improved strategic transport links and telecommunications , have facilitated a net in-flow of population into rural areas over the past 25-30 years. While metropolitan areas suffered a 4.6 per cent decline in population between 1981 and 1991, rural areas saw a rise of 10.2 per cent. As well as increasing the demand for goods and services locally, the incomers have brought additional entrepreneurial and technical skills, as well as capital for investment. The education level of people living in rural areas is now marginally higher than the national average even though the population profile is significantly older. There is also some evidence of the out-migration of younger people probably in search of jobs, training and affordable housing. It is an objective of policy to reverse this population exchange and to restore the age profile of rural areas to one closer to the national profile.

Income and work patterns

Average weekly wages are lower in the more remote English counties than elsewhere and there is much low-paid casual work undertaken in rural areas, particularly linked to agriculture and tourism. The proportion of part-time jobs and self employment is both higher than the national average and growing at a faster rate. On the other hand, the female participation is lower in rural areas than the national average, reflecting the lack of employment opportunities for women in rural areas and the lack of child care provision.

Rural enterprise

Small firms are the main engine of wealth and employment creation and are particularly important in rural areas where the opportunities for large inward investment projects are generally not forthcoming or practical. Self employment is much higher in rural areas, which to some extent reflects the predominance of one-person and very small businesses in the countryside and the influence of family farming and agricultural contract labour. New firms in both urban and rural areas tend to be founded by people living in the locality, although research shows that most new firm founders had moved to the countryside prior to setting up the firm. In remote areas there is evidence to suggest that a significant minority of small firm start-ups were by people specifically in-migrating to start their business, attracted to the areas by quality of life considerations. Rural companies in general count pleasant environment, good labour relations and lower wage costs among the benefits of a rural location. Skills shortages and lack of training facilities were among the disadvantages.

Planning and development in the countryside

Planning policy for the countryside is aimed at encouraging economic development while at the same time conserving local natural environments. Conflict can arise as society balances the need for expansion of jobs in rural areas with a desire to protect the amenities and cultural heritage of the countryside. England is a heavily populated country and there is a strong popular movement to conserve the countryside and resist development or re-development in rural areas. The UK government strategy on sustainable development aims, among other things, to reduce pollution and congestion arising from commuting by car and advocates the co-location of jobs and homes. In rural areas the application of this policy will encourage small towns and villages to become more self-sustaining in economic and social terms as well as environmental.

National government policy

The recent OECD Jobs Study acknowledged that rural employment strategies should be related to national employment policies, taking account of macroeconomic conditions. The OECD Group of the Council on Rural Development paper "Government Measures for Rural Employment Creation" suggested four policies that were of particular importance for rural job creation:

40

enhancing the functioning of the labour markets; nurturing an entrepreneurial climate; improving labour force skills and competence; and enhancing the creation and diffusion of technology. These are all active areas for UK government policy. Greater labour market flexibility has been a policy objective throughout the 1980s and 1990s. It is effected by a programme of deregulation and the promotion of enterprise. A recent survey of a number of key indicators on wages and employment points to an increase in flexibility, *e.g.* more part-time, self employment and temporary work and more functional flexibility at workplaces. Initiatives to encourage self employment and the reform of tax and social security policies are aimed at removing disincentives to work and improving labour flexibility and mobility. Active labour market policies are pursued through the twin routes of the Employment Service, which helps unemployed people compete in the labour market; and training and enterprise programmes, which are targeted at key populations in the economy, including the unemployed and the small-scale entrepreneur. Various special arrangements exist for the unemployed in rural areas relating to help with transport, the provision of job vacancy information, distance learning packs and mobile job centres.

Small firms are a key target population for the provision of government assistance and advice. A network of local Business Links has been established to improve the competitiveness of small firms and provide a single point of access to tap into a wide range of business support services. These include a technology and innovation service, which helps small and medium sized firms understand the importance of innovation, solve technical problems and identify relevant new technologies. In rural areas the RDC is an active partner in the Business Link network.

There are skill shortages in rural areas which can prevent small firms from achieving their potential growth. Skills training is delivered through a network of private sector led Training and Enterprise Councils (TECs). A consortium of 28 rural TECs addresses the rural dimension of their programmes and co-operates in programme development. Delivery of training has a higher unit cost in rural areas because of the dispersed and relatively small target population. Some research indicates that the uptake of training is often lower in rural areas than urban. Rural firms, employees and the unemployed are located further away from training providers than their urban counterparts. In addition, small firms, which predominate in rural areas, are less likely than larger businesses to have the resources to identify training needs, to provide them in-house, or to afford the down-time in releasing staff for external training. The development of flexible learning and skills in teleworking are training initiatives particularly relevant to rural areas and small firms. By providing support for enterprises and encouraging the local provision of skills training, it is possible both to attract and retain skilled workers in rural areas.

Rural development programmes

In addition to national programmes, the RDC is the Government's principal agency for rural development in England. Its mandate covers the whole country but most of its direct assistance is targeted on the RDAs in the more disadvantaged and peripheral rural areas. In each of its RDAs the RDC brings together the local authorities and other agencies, including public, private and voluntary sectors, to assess local needs and opportunities in the areas and to develop integrated strategies and programmes for dealing with them. The emphasis is on improving the climate and general infrastructure to enable local enterprise to flourish. Highly focused financial support is provided for these integrated rural development programmes, and also targeted at individual enterprises in the form of business advice, loans and grants.

The RDC also operates support for local partnership projects under a competitive Rural Challenge bidding process. An important element in the RDC's work is the provision of workspace for small firms either through the provision of new factory units or offices or the grant-aiding of the re-use of existing rural buildings. The RDC's philosophy is based on the premise that strengthening indigenous enterprise will be more successful in the long-term than trying to attract large scale inward investment. In addition, rural areas will be more sustainable if they can support local jobs and services which reduce the need to travel or commute.

Conclusion

Many of the explicit aims of the OECD's Rural Development Programme are embraced by the UK's policy framework for rural employment. To make the most of limited government resources, effective targeting is increasingly important, both by population, like government policy towards small firms and the unemployed, and by location, like the RDC's Rural Development Areas. The UK government is currently re-examining its policies for rural areas and aims to issue White Papers (policy statements) for England and Scotland later this year. The Rural Development Commission is pressing for a strengthening of the rural dimension of policy formulation and national programme provision to secure better access for rural people, particularly in more remote areas, to good quality training and business support services and a wider range of employment opportunities.

Switzerland

Theoretical background: the theory of polarisation versus neo-classical theory

The theory of polarisation, which supports the thesis of the mobility of jobs, can be summarised as follows:

The mobility of the factors of production of capital, labour and innovation is selective in terms of quantity, quality and time. The most attractive centres drain off capital (the quantitative aspect), the best workers (qualitative aspect) and the most rapidly marketable innovations (time aspect) from the surrounding areas and hinterland. Even when these centres are expanding, the attraction they exert remains stronger than the forces of expansion. These centres are at an advantage not only because of their attractiveness, but also because of the inability of peripheral areas to attract development.

Neo-classical theory, on the other hand, supports the thesis of population mobility.

According to this theory, limited competition on all markets constitutes the basis of trade between regions. Workers are attracted by the highest wages. In rural regions whose population is dwindling, labour becomes scarce and valuable, while in regions with a rising population due to immigration, wages begin to fall. Conversely, capital flows towards regions that promise a high marginal rate of return on funds invested, which helps increase the well-being of peripheral areas.

Conclusion

According to the neo-classical approach, the best policy to counter the unequal development of regions is non-intervention (i.e., passive restructuring). The theory of polarisation, on the other hand, requires the active implementation of programmes, for it assumes that inequalities among regions are an inherent outcome of the interplay of market forces, and that these inequalities will be greater the poorer a country is.

Historical and empirical evidence: the case for and against these theories

Economic and historical studies bear out the basic principles of the polarisation thesis. Even highly developed countries have observed a continuous trend in this direction.

The authors of studies carried out in the framework of the national programme "Regional Problems in Switzerland" emphasised the selective nature of factor mobility as early as the 1980s. High value factors have a greater polarisation effect than other factors. Low value factors of production, in particular, are more strongly attracted by the expansion of the main agglomerations than by peripheral regions and regions dominated by small cities. In the short or medium term, the polarisation trends are nevertheless stronger than the expansion effects, which only become evident over the longer term.

During the past two decades in Switzerland, there was initially a dispersal of the population, as the distance between workers' homes and workplaces grew continuously. Later, this trend was followed by a dispersal of jobs, which were transferred from city centres to the wider zone of influence of agglomerations.

The consequences of territorial development through mobility

Industrialised countries have benefited greatly from social and economic mobility. It is because of this mobility that the problem of regions was not a major policy issue in our country for a considerable time.

Furthermore, high mobility generates costs for the economy as a whole (negative externalities) that emerge, among others, in the following ways:

– inadequate territorial development policies. In particular, one can point to the inequitable distribution of negative secondary effects among various regions and different segments of the population;

– a tendency to neglect local natural and human resources in favour of more distant ones;

– harm to the environment. Moreover, some ecological damage can have an impact on the life of future generations.

– Principles for a rural development policy

– Rural development policy must first of all pursue a long-term and sustainable strategy in favour of the mobility of jobs. The justification for this policy is that it encompass the needs of the economy and society as a whole, and, as a result, it must be based on criteria that reflect these higher interests;

– this approach is difficult to put into practice as long as the relevant policies and programmes are based solely on the concept of equity. An economy is not only efficient because its exporters, importers and the enterprises operating on its domestic market are competitive (the functional approach), but also because it develops the potential of a country's regions (the territorial approach);

– this approach is also difficult to put into practice as long as the rules of the market do not apply to the amenities provided by rural regions, which have a value, but no price. Consequently, further measures should be taken to implement the conclusions of the work on rural amenities;

– even if the policies and programmes intended for rural areas (agricultural policy, regional policy, promotion of SMEs, tourism policy and environmental policy) are based on market economy criteria, they can still pursue the strategy of mobility of jobs;

– rural development policy does not exclude the strategy of population mobility, particularly as regards the promotion of skilled human capital (skill development).

– Policy mix models

Rural development strategy should be differentiated according to the type of regions in question by combining the main priority of promoting mobility of jobs with a supplemental policy of population mobility. The outline below illustrates this position, which we wish to propose for discussion.

Recommendations taken from the National Programme for Research on Regional Problems in Switzerland

Development prospects of region	Level of development of region	
	low	*high*
low prospects	– encouraging mobility; – redistribution among individuals.	– encouraging innovation; – redistribution among regional or local authorities.
high prospects	– developing infrastructure; – stimulating employment; – encouraging innovation; – reforms of federalism; – redistribution among regional and local authorities;	– internalisation of external effects.

Source: National Programme for Research on Regional Problems, Switzerland.

Consequently, as regards the most appropriate policy mix, Switzerland has reached similar conclusions to those of the OECD Rural Development Programme in the framework of the rural employment creation project.

References

BRUGGER, E.A. (1985), *Développement économique régional*, Lausanne.

BRUGGER, E.A., FREY, R.L. (1985), *Politique régionale en Suisse : buts, problèmes, expériences, réformes*, Lausanne.

DFTCE (Commissioned by Swiss Federal Department of Transport, Communications and Energy), (August 1994), *Mobilité en Suisse, rapport à l'intention de la Commision des transports et des télécommunications du Conseil des États*, Bern, Zurich.

FREY, R.L. (1985), *Politique régionale : une évaluation*, Lausanne.

OECD (1993), *What Future for Our Countryside? A Rural Development Policy*, Paris.

OECD (1994), *Creating Rural Indicators for Shaping Territorial Policy*, Paris.

OECD (1994), *The Contribution of Amenities to Rural Development*, Paris.

OECD, (1995), *Creating Employment for Rural Development. New Policy Approaches*, Paris.

CHAPTER 5   A STRONGER ECONOMIC BASE FOR
RURAL AREAS: SPECIALISATION VERSUS DIVERSIFICATION

Canada

The sectoral diversification question

Economic diversity was more common in rural areas when labour markets were local and rural communities had a more self-sustaining economic base. The expansion of trade due to improvements in transportation and communications led to increasing specialisation in single resource areas focusing on larger and usually external markets. Today, rural areas are generally viewed as economies specialising in traditional resource based industries (agriculture, forestry, mineral extraction or fishing) despite the fact that in many areas there is considerable diversity of economic activity.

Rural areas are subject to the same forces that are driving economic change in the national economy. Continuous pressures to improve competitiveness and to compete in global markets will continue to increase substitution of capital for labour in traditional resource industries and as such these industries are not expected to provide major sources of new employment.

Specialisation in many rural economies has made them particularly vulnerable to business cycles and resource depletion. The collapse of the ground fish industry in Atlantic Canada is a significant example of the impact of resource depletion on a sectoral-dependent rural economy. While the future of some Atlantic rural communities affected by the decline may still lie in the fisheries-related activities, others are seeking new types of enterprises and livelihoods.

Decline in employment in traditional sectors has led to the encouragement of diversification as one economic strategy for rural areas. A significant trend in recent years in agricultural households in many OECD countries has been diversification of income from pluriactivity, whereby some household members are employed in off-farm work. This raises the question as to what is the appropriate target for a diversification strategy in rural areas: the region, the rural community, the household or the individual within a household?

Traditional resource industries will undoubtedly remain the economic base of many rural areas for years to come and building on existing resource use and skills is seen as one means of sustaining many rural economies. Even where further exploiting a comparative advantage by specialisation is strong, however, there are risks in a global market. Diversification strategies often emerge from within sectors and focus on creating new, value-added opportunities within the sector. In Canada, for example, within the agriculture sector, producers are encouraged to diversify their enterprise mix and to explore further value-added processing and niche market development related to agriculture. Research is focused on finding new products from agricultural resources. Similar diversification strategies are being pursued in the forestry and fisheries sector. Strategies that entrench sectoral dependence create greater economic stability only if the new value added base is less price sensitive than the traditional production activity.

A comprehensive diversification strategy fosters the development of activities both related and not related to the existing dominant industry. If diversification is encouraged based on competitive advantage, the small size and limited resource base of most rural areas makes it difficult for them to assemble a critical mass of skills and resources to be a competitive producer of more than one or two goods or services. The only competitive advantage may in fact lie in the further development of their existing resource base. In many rural areas, tourism is seen to offer potential as a new source of development based on exploitation of local resources, scenic, cultural or historic attributes sometimes in association with the traditional industry as in farm based tourism.

High growth sectors in the rural economy in recent decades have been in manufacturing and services (though in Canada rural manufacturing has not been a growth area in terms of employment over the last decade). Much manufacturing activity has also been linked to the traditional resource sectors. In many of the older industrial economies, manufacturing activity has also been linked to the traditional resource sectors. In many of the older industrial economies, manufacturing activity is increasingly going "off-shore" attracted by the low labour costs in developing economies. How rural areas in the industrial economies adapt their economic base to remain competitive depends in part on their ability to find new products and services in which to specialise and to develop niche markets in which they can maintain a competitive advantage. How far rural areas should be encouraged to seek new types of business enterprises not associated with their traditional sectoral dependence or whether an economic strategy predominantly related to the major resource sector still remains the more viable long term future for many rural areas is an important question. However, such a strategy should be referred to as diversification or micro-specialisation.

Information technology as a rural development tool

The emergence of services as the major growth sector in both urban and rural areas of most OECD countries and the increasing role of information technology in all aspects of life, both economic and social, have profound implications for the future of development of rural areas and for the specialisation vs. diversification choice of rural economies.

Information technology can overcome the diseconomies of distance allowing rural areas to participate in the new information economy. The challenge for rural areas is how to access new technology and develop skills to take advantage of such technology for the generation of wealth and for the maintenance of quality of life. Modern information technology can enable rural communities to establish new and more broadly diversified economies as well as enhancing diversification within their traditional resource base. Rural areas can utilise opportunities generated by information technology in three major ways:

1. As producers of high tech goods and services

– through the creation of employment directly related to technology development such as the design and production of new technology applications (e.g. development of software and specialised information services);

– service provision using information technology (e.g. outsourcing of computer based work, mail order processing, data entry and telemarketing).

Studies of high technology goods and services suggest that they are subject to significant agglomeration effects and that rural areas are for the most part unlikely to be primary locations for these industries. Rural areas could become increasingly peripheral to the information economy as providers of high tech goods and service unless new niche market opportunities are fostered and developed.

Information services development and provision need not be site specific, though the ability of rural areas to capture such business depends on their capacity to market their services and to show that they have the necessary skills to undertake the work. Telecentres in Newfoundland and telecottages throughout many European countries provide examples of such direct use of information technology, though evaluations to date have shown that such centres have generated relatively few jobs.

As the use of information technology becomes incorporated into rural areas, the demand for rural-specific services and information may itself become a market opportunity.

2. *As users of high tech goods and services:* as an enabling tool information technology can help strengthen a diversification strategy by enabling access to information on existing and new markets, stimulating innovation and product differentiation, and providing opportunities for greater networking. The development of horizontal and vertical linkages and integration through electronic networks can strengthen market involvement and help rural businesses and rural communities to overcome business size and market access problems. So called "virtual companies" can exist in rural as well as urban areas.

3. *To maintain and enhance quality of life:* information technology can affect the social and cultural life of rural communities. Advances in telemedicine, health care and services provision, and developments in interactive and a-synchronous distance education and training, all have major implications for the quality of life in rural communities. The desire of rural people, particularly youth, to remain in place or return to a rural community, and that of newcomers to be attracted by amenities of rural areas can be enhanced through the information technology.

Rural realities

1. *Access to information technology is not universal:* often the more peripheral a rural area the greater the limitations of access whether through lack of basic infrastructure, regulatory barriers or distance related tariff structures. The small market size of rural populations may not attract private sector investment in basic infrastructure development. The regulatory regime may

prevent other service providers from entering the market, and distance related tariff structures can contribute to the higher costs of doing business from a rural area.

2. *Inappropriate skills in rural areas:* there is a growing mismatch between the rural worker skills and those required for jobs using new technology. Network literacy, the ability to identify, access, and use electronic information will be critical skills in the new information economy. Current trends in the nature of employment suggest that high wage jobs in expanding sectors will be under represented in rural areas because of the inadequate skills of the rural labour force.

3. *Information technology can eliminate jobs as well as create them:* the introduction of information technology in rural areas can reduce employment by substituting on-line information and services for previous direct service provision. The jury is still out on the net balance between loss of jobs and potential growth of employment.

The territorial dimension

Problems of diversification and alternative employment opportunities are generally magnified by community size and remoteness. Sectoral specialisation and population density vary region by region, as do distance and location relative to urban markets. All combine to create different potentials and responses among rural areas.

Economically integrated rural areas are generally more diversified. The development and application of new technology in such areas may closely parallel developments in adjacent urban centres. Rural entrepreneurs located near urban areas can more readily grasp opportunities to provide telematic services to urban clients. In addition, increasing numbers of urban residents are seeking the quality of life provided in rural environments as location in which to live and from which to conduct business. Some large corporations facing major restructuring are also examining the development of satellite offices in adjacent rural areas to respond to the quality of life demands of executives and their families. Satellite offices and the growth of telecommuting can introduce new wealth and skills to rural communities adjacent to urban centres.

Intermediate areas and remote rural areas: while economically integrated rural areas can link into the financial, marketing and high technology services of their urban neighbours, more distant areas may continue to be at a relative disadvantage. In such areas the long-term value of information technology may be more in the use made of the technology to foster other economic and social development rather than in the direct production of associated high tech goods and services.

Role of Government

If access to information technology is a key to future participation in the global economy, the question can be raised as to what is the appropriate role for government in ensuring universal access to the technology.

Access related issues of infrastructure provision, regulations and tariff structures can all be influenced by government policy. In the Canadian context basic infrastructure provision is largely in the hands of the private sector and as such the ability to access information technology varies throughout the country. The role of a number of provincial governments has been significant in fostering access. For example, in the province of New Brunswick the infrastructure development has provided connectivity to all rural and urban areas throughout the province. Considerable federal government funding has been dedicated to the advancement of the information highway with one of the major long term goals of universal access. For some rural areas accessibility may be based on social equity rather than economic considerations.

Ensuring availability of training and education to improve skills in the use of new technology is another important role of government. In the Canadian context while education is largely a provincial responsibility, one example of the federal government role has been in facilitating the development of the SchoolNet program that has the objective of linking all schools to Internet and providing a range of on-line information services through the schools. A more recent access to 1 000 rural and remote communities over the next three to four years. At the community level, the emergence of Freenets and community electronic networks is a notable development in Canada. Initially an urban phenomenon, community networks, organised and managed by local people are now being developed in rural areas and offer another point of access to information and knowledge sharing among rural communities.

Government also has a role to play in ensuring that on-line access to information on its programmes and services is available to rural as well as urban areas. In addition, on the research side, by examining the relationship between information technology and the generation of jobs and wealth in rural areas, the government can help to determine if investment in information technology is cost effective or if it must be supported on equity considerations.

Japan

Rural Japan

Characteristics

The forested area of Japan is very large, covering almost 70 per cent of the total land area, and most of it is hilly or mountainous. Flatland accounts for a relatively small area, with all the major cities located there.

Flatland rural areas, approximately equivalent to the economically integrated areas in the OECD rural typology, are defined as the "hinterland" of cities and are integrated in the urban economy. The demand for non-agricultural land is very high in Japan. As land resources are very scarce, the main policy issue for flattened rural areas revolves around the formulation of appropriate land use control.

Hilly and mountainous areas, which approximate remote areas in the OECD rural typology, suffer from an ageing and decreasing population. Local cities are assumed to be the development centres of these areas but in fact their economic influence is relatively low. The main policy issue here concerns appropriate land use management and economic revitalisation towards a balanced nation-wide development.

Basic development directions

– Flatland rural areas: from an agricultural point of view, it is important to stimulate the farming sector's profitability and hence development through economies of scale. From a non-agricultural point of view, the Government can only play a limited role by inviting new companies to these rural areas. Governmental efforts should instead be directed towards a reconciliation between rural development and environmental conservation in flatland areas;

55

– hilly and mountainous areas: except in some cases of specialised production, agriculture is less economically efficient than other industries as topographic constraints make economies of scale difficult. Similarly, inviting new companies (other than R&D-intensive enterprises) to operate in these areas is unlikely to be successful due to the high transportation costs involved. Rural development must therefore be endogenous rather than exogenous. As in the case of the "one special product for each village" programme in Oita prefecture, all kinds of local resources (e.g. agricultural products, local heritage, natural amenities, etc.) should be mobilised to create job opportunities. Improvement of the infrastructure is a prerequisite to resource mobilisation;

– agriculture as a base for sustainable rural development: as well as its function of controlling water flows and soil erosion, agricultural land also provides space for amenities. From the viewpoint of sustainability, agriculture is a basic industry in the process of rural development.

Specialisation or diversification

There exist significant differences among rural areas in terms of the economy, society and environment, as mentioned above. These differences need to be examined when discussing policy issues. This is also true when discussing which of the two development paths, "specialisation" or "diversification", should be chosen for a given rural area. The following are some points to be considered in deciding on development paths for rural areas:

– Specialisation is not possible for all rural areas. It is conditional upon certain factors such as market access. By nature, specialisation requires a large initial capital outlay and highly-skilled labour. This therefore limits its application to areas where economic activities in the private sector are already vigorous and to firms which already benefit from a sufficient accumulation of capital, land and skilled labour;

– diversification will be resilient to market changes in the economy as a whole but individual markets will often be volatile;

– there is a risk in relocating firms to rural areas without careful planning, as their survival is not fully guaranteed. Local populations have an unstable income source in this case and rural areas lose out if the firms then leave;

- in most parts of the hilly and mountainous areas, a "diversification" programme usually has a better chance of success in the medium/long term than a "specialisation" programme. Specialisation is expensive and a risk is involved in the shift of technology and labour. Nevertheless, the establishment of networks between SMEs is one of the key factors to success. This makes it possible for these areas to be sufficiently competitive in order to respond to market changes and consumer demands;

- new technological development will contribute to the development path of both specialisation and diversification to different degrees. Bio-technology for example, is used in the development of high value-added agricultural products as in the case of specialisation, and also for food industries to help their diversification;

- in the case of computer networks, until the 1970s, a so-called "centralised system" was favoured, whereas now a "decentralised system" is gradually evolving, which could help to overcome problems of distance and low population density in rural areas in the near future.

Taking the above points into consideration, the following table attempts to categorise the elements necessary for specialisation and diversification when rural areas (or firms) are faced with the choice between the two development paths. The farming sector is treated separately as one of the major actors in the rural economy.

Rural areas need economic incentives to help them decide whether to specialise or diversify, or a mixture of the two. This presents a challenge for government decision makers at different levels who are responsible for designing rural policies. One fact which is certain is that neither a single-for-all nor a specific-for-each policy can be applied with success. The role of the Government is, accordingly, to create an economic and perhaps social environment in which rural areas can take the initiative for their own development. The decision as to which path rural areas should follow finally depends on the best allocation of their resources.

Factors influencing Japan's choice to specialise or diversify

	Specialisation	Diversification
Rural Economy	– High technology developments; – Education and skills; – Designation of enterprise zones;	– Communication and information networks; – Participation of different actors; – marketing and advertising; – Rural tourism.
Farm Economy	– Bio-technology development; – Marketing knowledge; – Economies of scale in farming.	– Agri-businesses; – Up and downstream industries; – Rural and urban communication.

Source: Ministry of Agriculture, Forestry and Fisheries, Japan.

Rural policy challenge

In Japan, several ministries are involved in rural development issues. The Ministry of Agriculture, Forestry and Fisheries, among others, play an important role as a leading authority on rural development. The Ministry's rural policy covers various aspects which accommodate rural needs and provides incentives for the rural population to take initiatives in its development.

The rural policies listed below are linked to the development of specialisation or diversification in varying degrees, although they were not specifically designed as such.

Policies for:

1. agriculture as an attractive lifetime career:

   – development of economies of scale for farming;

   – promotion of value-added products;

   – improvement of infrastructure;

2. agribusiness development (in particular, resource-based development):

   – a well-planned programme of enterprise location based on industry promotion laws for rural areas;

   – provision of processing facilities;

3. encouraging rural tourism:

   – development of the market for rural assets such as landscape, culture and heritage;

   – provision of necessary facilities such as accommodation;

4. R&D intensive industries:

   – a location plan for R&D-intensive industries based on the policy of accelerating regional development based on high-technology industrial complexes;

5. improvement of rural living conditions:

   – horizontal policy co-operation between different ministries;

   – special investment in hilly and mountainous areas;

6. human resources development and technology development:

   – facilitation of R&D new technologies through joint efforts and co-operation between government, research institutes and the private sector;

   – extension of new technologies;

   – training and skills management.

   Development potential varies between rural areas. The choice of path, be it "specialisation" or "diversification", rests on making the best use of natural, human and cultural resources. Rural policy should encompass measures which will provide appropriate conditions for the development of rural areas. Japan will continue to pursue such a rural policy.

CHAPTER 6   THE ROLES OF DIFFERENT PARTNERS

Spain

Introduction

In the 1960s, in the midst of its industrialisation, Spain found itself confronted with new problems involving its rural areas and deemed that those problems should be addressed at once, in the context of agricultural modernisation.

At the time, approaches to territorial development focused on centres of industrial expansion that would enable "agglomeration economies" to develop around selected cities. Government action was to take the form of investment incentives and the granting of certain tax breaks and territorial benefits.

In addition, agricultural policies endeavoured to make farming more profitable, and funds were earmarked to enhance the technical skills of the agricultural labour force. Measures such as these, with their focus on greater agricultural specialisation, were taken to stem the loss of farm jobs among people tempted by brighter employment prospects in the new industrial areas.

Later, in 1972, a development programme based on the growth pole model was implemented around "area capitals". The scheme designed to bring about a closer linkage between rural and urban area development. This initial system tied in with a new concept of land-use planning that mapped out geographical entities made up of numerous communes. It was to be implemented by the central government via new areas officially designated as "Land-Use Planning" or "Special Action" districts. The strategies pursued in those districts through joint action of the Ministries of Agriculture and the Interior drew upon programmes to intensify farm output that were co-ordinated with municipal procurement schemes.

In all, 412 "rural area capitals" were eligible for aid under the programme. Assistance was concentrated chiefly on rural-urban housing, modernisation of farms and agricultural support infrastructure (land consolidation and irrigation), as well as on other efforts relating to community facilities and basic infrastructure, especially in communes selected for their socio-economic viability.

Intervention by government or the private sector in the development of rural areas is no accident, but the result of analysing the development programmes carried out over recent years. Such analysis has clearly demonstrated that successful rural development programmes involve a certain "critical mass" -- demographically, economically and socially -- without which the investments they entail would produce no multiplier effects.

Intra-institutional co-ordination

In 1978, the Spanish constitution instituted regional autonomous governments ("Autonomous Communities"), further decentralising the State's administrative power but without eliminating its responsibilities in the areas of planning, co-ordination and, in some respects, management.

This scheme for regional autonomy has been instrumental in the formulation of a rural development policy. It has mobilised the resources of the government entities involved as well as the private sector and relevant organisations at local and regional level.

Rural development programmes and programmes to upgrade the facilities of rural communes, as well as the new administrative districts, were created by regional bodies on the basis of population and socio-economic viability. According to their capabilities and resources, regional authorities formulated development plans consistent with the nation's overall economic goals. Thus established, the plans were implemented via co-operation agreements with the State, in the form of conventions and instruments of consultation and agreement.

Because intra-institutional co-operation requires budgetary co-ordination between the central government departments concerned, an Interministerial Committee on Rural Development was set up. In addition to performing the central government's constitutional functions of planning and co-ordination, the Committee apportions funding for rural development programmes among ministries.

A number of Autonomous Communities have also established similar co-ordinating bodies. In some cases, the agricultural, industrial and commercial authorities have been merged into single Steering Centres, likewise in order to optimise action and resource allocation throughout the Community.

The State's primary role at central level is to formulate a National Framework Plan for Rural Development, setting broad objectives for rural areas and determining the phases of consultation with the Autonomous Communities.

Inter-institutional co-operation

Autonomous Communities have their own funding for regional and rural development programmes. In addition, they can access the resources of mutual savings banks, whose dedication to community interests is written into their charter through a requirement that local and regional public institutions be represented on their boards; such banks are therefore social as well as financial institutions.

Regional Development Plans, which the Autonomous Communities draw up in connection with EU structural policy (covering regions that, from a structural standpoint, are below the European Union average), also contribute to territorial development, e.g. by improving communications facilities or means of transport. The Plans are formulated as part of a transregional planning scheme, responsibility for which lies with the State. For its part, the central government apportions funding between the various administrative departments and regional programmes.

Co-ordination with local agents

Rural development draws upon local initiatives, inhabitants and organisations.

Municipalities and other local entities play an active role in planning facilities and infrastructure. These plans are co-ordinated with regional programmes and take account of the investment needs of municipalities in different types of rural areas: integrated economic areas, intermediate areas and remote areas. They are financed at central and local government levels.

Since 1991, responsibility for rural development has been predominantly in the hands of local people and associations, i.e. development has been largely "bottom-up".

Accordingly, aid has been provided by the European Union's LEADER programmes. These 52 programmes allow the Rural Development Groups greater autonomy and enable new initiatives to be taken. They are managed by public and private institutions at local level, including chambers of commerce, chambers of agriculture, co-operatives, employers' associations, special interest groups and municipal unions. These institutions establish their own relationships with the central and regional governments. Among their activities are the development of endogenous resources, tourism (which accounts for over 30 per cent of local initiatives), small industrial enterprises and new agricultural undertakings. Once it has been decided which activities are to be developed, these bodies function completely independently, with respect to both implementation and subsequent supervision.

While creating programmes for endogenous development is effective, such programmes need to be co-ordinated with other development initiatives. Supervisory Committees for Regional and Rural Development Programmes have therefore been set up, in particular to ensure that action is taken in compliance with established timetables. These committees will act alongside central and regional authorities, municipalities and local task forces. The committees' work is based on Framework Programmes, which constitute the common reference for all parties concerned and all agreements that are signed.

United States

Introduction

The topic of this paper, "The Roles of Different Partners", implies a consensus that rural development policy should be shaped and carried out in partnership. A partnership which comprises all levels of government, local entrepreneurs, and people, as individuals and in groups, is indeed necessary. The difficult questions concern the nature of that partnership; how to maximise the value of each partner's contributions and sometimes more important, how to encourage the entry of new partners into the process. It is tempting from the perspective of the Federal (U.S. national) government to try to elaborate a grand design for the partnership, scripting the role of each partner. And indeed it is inevitable that we have expectations of our partners. But a true partnership is mutual; it cannot be defined and managed by one of the partners. Therefore this paper will focus on what is the role of the Federal government and how can national government be a better partner ?

Rural diversity

The proper role for the Federal government in rural development is grounded in the circumstances of the challenge. As the Group of the Council's report *What Future for Our Countryside? A Rural Development Policy* notes of Member countries, the most salient feature of American rural areas is their striking diversity. Some are thriving; some are quietly prosperous; some are stagnating economically; some are poor; some have comparatively high average incomes, but are losing population; some depend on agriculture; some are urbanising; some are undergoing environmental degradation, while still others are being "gentrified". But almost all have substantially developed human resources. Local officials, leaders, entrepreneurs, civic associations and many others are customarily partners for development in rural communities. There are some communities where this is not as true, where for reasons of historic racial or cultural discrimination, there is little civic tradition and limited capacity to act as a community. Such communities are a special concern of the Federal government to which we have responded in a special way. The great challenge is how and to whom the Federal government provides assistance for development which is appropriate to the great range of rural circumstances.

Layered, fragmented Federal programs

Almost as varied as rural communities are the assistance programs currently administered by the Federal government. A recent General Accounting Office (GAO -- the Congressional evaluation agency) report refers to 828 Federal programs which serve rural communities (many of which also serve larger places); 689 of these they describe as developmental programs. The form of delivery of these Federal programs usually reflects the emphasis of the era in our history in which they were conceived. Programs such as those administered by the Corps of Engineers (major public works) and the Bureau of Indian Affairs (administration of reservations) mostly originated in our frontier past, when the rural population was very sparse and local communities had few resources available for public purposes. These "Frontier" programs are top-down, administered centrally, and largely ignore local institutions and capacities.

"Storehouse" programs, designed to promote economic development by facilitating the extraction of rural resources -- agricultural, mineral, and gradually, human resources, began about 100 years ago. Most of the US agricultural, industrial incentive, and infrastructure programs fall in this category. These programs are still the most numerous and involve the bulk of

Federal spending in rural areas. Except for the agricultural programs, they typically involve a contribution of Federal funds for a specific activity administered by a local government. A third category, "Poor House" programs, was added during the Depression in the 1930s and more such programs were created during the War on Poverty in the 1960s. They are administered in a partnership much like the Storehouse programs. Recently, "Backyard" programs have been added. They treat rural areas as zones for urban recreation rather than targets for economic development. Generally, they are another set of top down programs which basically impose mandates on rural and governments.

Our Federal government through several department and agencies administers the hundreds of similar, overlapping, or duplicated programs -- programs for four basic purposes, with separate eligibility requirements, application forms and procedures, conditions, and matching requirements. They are a cake stacked in layers or a pudding with several apparently unrelated themes. As the GAO report puts it, U.S. rural development programs suffer from the lack of a clear strategic vision. It is no wonder that local officials complain about the difficulties of accessing and using these programmes in a reasonable, coherent local development strategy.

Providing a strategic vision

The US Federal government is working to be a better partner, first by developing a strategic vision and second by making Federal programs more accessible and adaptable to local needs and priorities. The Federal government cannot solve the problems of rural America but it can assist in developing and implementing solutions that are inclusive of all people and meet the needs unique to the great diversity of situations. The Federal government is trying to build the rural development efforts of USDA upon the local leadership and capacity that exists throughout the country. In a limited number of cases, where it is necessary, the Federal government is also actively seeking to encourage the development of local capacities.

The new Federal role in rural development is to assist communities, based on inclusive development initiatives, to become more competitive in a world marketplace through creating sustainable economic opportunities for all residents. To achieve this, the Federal government now has three priorities for its rural development efforts. They are: *(i)* reduction of long-term poverty in the approximately 500 poorest rural counties (of a total of 2 300) in the United States; *(ii)* increasing the viability of rural communities with declining populations and job opportunities; and *(iii)* assistance for those parts of rural America experiencing short-term difficulty from rapid structural change due to shifts in public policy, the international marketplace or natural disasters.

Within the three priority areas, emphasis is on those initiatives which have the greatest potential impact and those which represent the most opportunity for demonstration, experimentation, and learning. USDA rural development initiatives will work co-operatively with other Federal agencies, non-profit and for-profit private groups, tribal, state and local governments. Co-operative ventures will be designed to create innovative approaches to providing physical infrastructure, ensuring the health and well-being of all rural people and stimulating business enterprises in order to provide employment and ownership opportunities.

Co-ordination without authority?

GAO's remedy for the problems of program delivery it describes so well is more multi-agency, cross-departmental co-ordination. The report suggests the creation of an interagency working group on rural development made up of representatives of several agencies. Almost everything called for in this regard replicates responsibilities already granted to the Secretary of Agriculture under the Rural Development Policy Act of 1980. Similar calls for and efforts at multi-agency co-ordination and co-operation can be found in studies and legislation back to the 1930s. But the report encourages the view that all we need is a little will and a new mechanism.

Unfortunately the history of cross-departmental, multi-agency government co-operation and co-ordination is not nearly as encouraging. There have been many studies on the history of American rural development policy and the success of co-ordination over the last forty years. All conclude that co-operation and co-ordination are not enough. The literature suggests that the granting of *responsibility* without commensurate *authority* typically fails. A careful reading of the OECD Rural Public Management and Rural Development Program reports over the last decade offers no models over the last decade offers no models among Member countries where co-ordination without authority has been enough.

Alternative approaches to the delivery of Federal assistance

There are logical alternatives to making the Federal government a better rural development partner through more and better co-ordination of its programs. One would be to create a Department of Rural Development and consolidate in it the functions that are currently spread throughout a large number of Federal agencies and departments. A secretary of Rural Development would have the *authority* and *responsibility* to integrate and rationalise most of the Federal activities that touch rural people. That is a very appealing approach.

Another approach, the one currently being pursued is to re-examine and perhaps recreate the intergovernmental relationships which under-gird the rural development partnership. One aspect of this approach is to build an explicit rural development partnership with state governments. Partnership agreements have been negotiated with governors of 39 of the 50 states. These states have created state rural development councils which include Federal and state officials, local government officials, tribal representatives, financial and business leaders, and a range of other partners unique to each state. USDA and other Federal agencies are working more closely than ever before with state officials, and the private and non-profit sectors, to co-ordinate rural development efforts at the state level.

The Administration is also now proposing to Congress a Performance Partnership. This legislation would transform the current menu of rural development programs administered by the Department of Agriculture into an integrated initiative that would:

- consolidate many of the existing programs;

- make all the programs more flexible so that investments will more effectively meet local needs;

- re-invent implementation and increase reliance on measures of results; and

- involve all of the partners in the development of State strategic plans.

Under this proposal the funds for 14 of the major programs administered by USDA would be allocated by State. There, USDA State Rural Development Directors, in consultation with appropriate officials of the state government, could re-allocate funds among the programs according to the State's own priorities.

For some of the poorest rural communities, those which need to build more inclusive local leadership and community institutions at the same time they pursue economic development; a demonstration program of empowerment zones and enterprise communities have just been launched. Selected competitively on the basis of need, demonstrated effort to unite the community around popularly developed goals, and ability to secure the participation of a variety of partners, the three rural communities designated as empowerment zones will be given considerable Federal financial help and unique flexibility in the use of Federal programs administered by several departments. This program is similar in some regards to the French *contrat de plan*. Thirty enterprise communities will be given similar assistance but on a much smaller scale.

A wider partnership

Developing a strategic vision of the Federal role and better delivery of services are important steps but they do not exhaust our contributions as a rural development partner. Monumental changes are re-shaping economic geography in the OECD countries. The much described globalisation of economies has had a profound effect on rural areas. The indicators work of the Rural Development Program has given us the ability to begin systematically documenting that effect for the first time. I believe there are other, less visible but equally important currents at work. And there are certainly policy and program experiments underway in virtually every country represented at this meeting. One of the jobs of the Federal partner is to support and participate in forums such as the OECD program in order to help identify economic currents, understand their implications, learn from the experiences of others, and transmit that information. And since those on the Group of the Council and those who represent their countries at this meeting share that role in one way or another, this is truly a meeting of the international rural development partnership.

I will spend a final moment on what I think is one of the most important trends for rural areas. It is the growing recognition of importance of the quality of life, including ecological and aesthetic concerns. As rural areas continue to lose jobs in the traditional resource extraction industries on which they have long depended, it is essential that they find new ways to capture the economic value of the resources in which they abound. This seems to me to fit very nicely with the great change from an industrial to a post-industrial economic base which is taking place in most of the highly developed countries. That is why we attach so much importance to the Group's pioneering work on marketable (largely tourism) and non-marketable (merit goods) amenities. And why we are also concerned that the OECD budget in the future provide the resources necessary to continue this work as well as the work on employment generally.

Mexico

In the past, programmes for rural development and poverty alleviation in Mexico were designed and financed by the central government, following a typical "Top-Down" approach. At the beginning of the previous administration (1988-1994), such programmes started to change, giving more importance to community initiatives and decisions, and less weight to the imposition of ideas coming from the offices of the central government. In 1989 the Solidarity Programme was created under these guidelines, and since then, it represents the core element of the government's social policy (see table below). One of the main contributions of this programme has been the new relationship between the society at large and the government in carrying out policies for welfare improvement.

Solidarity is a national poverty alleviation programme that operates along three general lines:

- provision of public services for improving social welfare;

- regional development;

- support for agriculture production in communal lands.

The programme is based around four main principles:

- respect for the initiatives of individuals and communities;

- full and effective participation through the organisation of civil society;

- joint responsibility of government and beneficiaries;

- transparency, honesty and efficiency in handling the resources.

The main programmes of Solidarity in Mexico
Millions of new pesos

		Type of program (1)	1989 (2)	1990 (2)	1991 (2)	1992 (2)	1993 (2)	1994 (3)
1.	Health and Dignified Hospital	W	106,1	253,5	255,0	279,6	274,5	356,9
2.	Educational Infrastructure	W	122,7	169,9	237,0	300,0	248,9	311,5
3.	Children in Solidarity	W	--	--	145,0	378,9	606,4	840,3
4.	Sports facilities	W	3,9	37,9	79,9	110,9	141,2	124,3
5.	Dignified School	W	--	108,7	188,1	193,3	219,7	212,5
6.	Drinking water and sewerage	W	357,9	161,2	547,5	789,3	877,6	1079,7
7.	Electrification	W	90,6	173,9	267,8	295,4	265,8	363,2
8.	Dignified Housing	W	21,3	48,9	89,1	73,2	212,5	320,7
9.	Young People in Solidarity	W	39,5	63,7	130,3	187,5	304,8	178,9
10.	Women in Solidarity	P	10,9	18,2	31,7	41,8	39,7	40,5
11.	Productive support infrastructure	P	74,4	101,9	143,9	213,1	150,6	138,6
12.	Urbanisation	P	96,4	208,0	380,3	618,0	840,5	923,6
13.	Solidarity's micro-enterprises fund	P	--	--	--	406,7	361,0	108,1
14.	Solidarity Production fund	P	--	395,4	378,6	445,8	582,1	617,5
15.	Regional development programs	RD	#	#	#	#	#	#
16.	Rural roads and highways	RD	285,9	373,4	747,7	848,3	733,6	949,2
17.	Solidarity's municipal funds	RD	--	258,4	319,7	522,6	669,2	922,7
18.	Others	RD	430,4	907,4	1244,0	1287,7	1730,9	1736,0
TOTAL			1640,0	3277,4	5185,8	6992,1	8259,0	9232,2

Notes:
1. P = Productive; RD = regional Development; W = Welfare.
2. Exercised resources.
3. Estimated close.
= The spending is not cumulative. It is incorporated in the normal programs.

Source: Sexto Informe de Gobierno, Mexico, 1994.

The most important feature in the functioning of the programme is the full participation of local authorities and local population, and can also be considered as the main determinant of its success in rural areas. Indigenous groups and peasant committees involved in all stages of the projects and are responsible for their operation. Such committees draw on the tradition of co-operation among communities. The members of the Solidarity Committees are elected democratically in public assemblies and are directly accountable to the community. Together with the public authorities and social organisations, they determine the projects to be carried out, when to start them, how long they will take, at what cost and the way in which financial resources will be recovered and reinvested. All these principles avoid vestiges of paternalism, populism and political conditioning.

The second level of decision is constituted by a Municipal Council (local council), headed by the Municipal President and composed of representatives of the communities. The council gathers the proposals of all the Solidarity committees and, according to the poverty level within the communities and the nature of the projects, it chooses those considered as a priority.

At a federal level, the Ministry of Social Development (SEDESOL) establishes norms and general procedures for the functioning of Solidarity. The ministry co-ordinates the participation of the different institutions and states in order to allocate federal and state resources.

The mechanism for sharing the cost and responsibilities of the projects makes the programme economically efficient, as it identifies the real demand for public services and projects for the community. The recipients adopt a more selective attitude when they have to bear costs and responsibilities. This is an essential characteristic of Solidarity's "Bottom-up" approach to social policy.

Since the beginning, Solidarity's budget has continually increased (see table below). In 1989, it represented 0.32 per cent of GDP. In 1994 it had reached 0.74 per cent of GDP. The same has occurred for total government social expenditure: in 1989 it constituted 6.17 per cent of GDP, whereas in 1994 it represented 10.10 per cent of GDP. During the last six years of GDP Solidarity allocated around 60 per cent of its resources towards rural areas. For this year, real social expenses are expected to maintain the level reached last year.

Today, Mexico is facing a severe economic crisis that imposes the adoption of stricter efficiency criteria in the use of resources for social development. In an unprecedented move, President Zedillo's government has reacted to these new conditions by giving more importance to the strengthening of local governments (municipalities), in the context of regional development.

The municipality is the ideal structure with which the government can establish a direct contact with the communities, since it represents the closest governmental unit to their problems and initiatives. The municipality is a territorial division composed of one or more communities with the legal authority to manage tributary and federal resources in the allocation of public services. Thus, the capacity of municipalities to manage resources has been improved, though it has to be recognised that in most of the cases the financial conditions in the provision of public services remain precarious.

Social and Solidarity spending in Mexico
Millions of new pesos and percentages

	1989	1990	1991	1992	1993	1994
Total Solidarity Spending	1 640	3 280	5 190	6 990	8 260	9 230
. Solidarity for Social Welfare	970	1 870	3 160	421	5 220	6 310
. Solidarity for production	170	880	990	1 560	1 870	1650
. Basic Infrastructure	310	470	890	1190	1 110	1220
. Other Programs	190	60	150	30	600	500
Solidarity spending as a share of GDP	0.32%	0.48%	0.60%	0.69%	0.73%	0.74%
Public Spending on social development (1)	31 330	44 420	66 720	88 010	106 990	126 220
Public Spending on social development as a share of GDP	6.17%	6.47%	7.71%	8.64%	9.49%	10.10%
Solidarity spending as a share of public spending on social development	5.23%	7.38%	7.77%	7.94%	7.72%	7.32%

1. Includes education, health care, regional and urban development.

Source: *Sexto Informe de Govierno*, Mexico, 1994.

In this way, real decentralisation efforts can be observed, which are added to the "Bottom-Up" approach of the social programmes. In this context, since 1995, Solidarity has taken new measures:

1. Solidarity will be composed of five funds that will replace several of the previous programmes: Solidarity's Municipal Fund, Indigenous Peoples' Development Fund, Social Groups Assistance Fund, Regional Development Promotion Fund and Solidarity's Micro-Enterprises Fund.

2. A group of priority regions will be supported with a higher level of resources. Such a group has been defined according to marginality and poverty criteria.

3. An Inter-Ministerial Commission of Social Development has been created in order to efficiently co-ordinate the activities of the agencies involved with social policy.

In order to strengthen the capacity of local governments to control the design and evaluation of social programmes, municipalities will be given at least 50 per cent of Solidarity's budget through the Solidarity's Municipal Fund Scheme. This programme has been defined following the "Bottom-Up" approach in order to benefit the poorest rural municipalities. It must be stressed that this fund is the most important among the five listed above.

CHAPTER 7   CO-ORDINATION OF POLICIES:
SECTORAL POLICY VERSUS TERRITORIAL POLICY

Austria

Factors for balance

Sectoral and territorial considerations are dimensions of any policy. The main factors that differentiate sectoral and territorial policies are their goals and results, rather than formal designations, institutional attributions or instruments employed. Sectoral and territorial aspects should be understood to be two poles between which policies move, being either defined as *ex ante* or interpreted as *ex post*. Understood thus, a primarily sectoral oriented subsidy programme might include a territorial component in varying the subsidy's conditions according to locations and regions, for example. At the other end of the scale one might have a subsidy programme, for example, that is only granted (exclusively) to selected locations and regions. In both cases we are dealing with *explicit territoriality*. *Implicit territoriality* may result from two situations: first, sectoral policies with measures that substantially modify the territorial situation, such as the expansion of a transportation network; second, the addressees of sectoral measures are only to be found in certain regions, as is the case of steel or textile industries.

Finally, it is important to note to what *level* of the administrative-political system the responsibility for certain sectoral measures belong. Territorial policy in the form of regional development planning will be different if it is worked out by a central government for regions than if the same task is carried out by the region itself.

Sectoral policy also has different effects depending on at what level it is implemented. If the provision of hospitals is the responsibility of a central government, the location structure will be different than if the task is carried out by the region (*Länder, Provinces* or *Kanton*) or municipality. The political distribution of power between the levels of administration of a country may thus play a significant role for the balance between the two poles of *sectoral* and *territorial* orientation.

The more responsibility the regions and municipalities have:

- the better represented are the interests of certain parts of areas; and

- the higher the need to achieve an equilibrium of interests.

If responsibility for territorial development exists on every level of the political-administrative system, then the instruments of territorial development planning are key to achieving this equilibrium.

The tension between sectoral and territorial policy is overlaid with the tension that exists between the individual levels of territorial interests. Territorial goals have to be enforced on every level though a "top-down" approach (the aim being *unity*) and a "bottom up" approach (the aim being *equilibrium*). Territorial policy at several levels, thus, usually requires both principles at the same time.

The impetus towards a "more territorial" view or approach might come on the one hand from the grass roots or local level, especially if the regional or local limits of an absolute strain (e.g. emissions) or of a relative disadvantage (e.g. available jobs) are surpassed. It might also come from the central government or administration if contradictions arise between the individual sectoral policies or if the unity of a common territory is endangered (these were the reasons for the initial "rise" of regional planning and now of spatial planning within the EU). Politically strong regions are very important for the implementation of territorially oriented policies.

Financial backing is a prerequisite to implement planning. Financial resources and legal powers of enforcement however, are becoming less and less suitable for implementing policies in the case of political resistance.

If the planning and the financing of measures are not organised in one institution then this is a handicap for the efficiency of a policy. In the case of territorial policies this means that the body responsible to implement the most important measures must have as a minimum the competence to carry out the accompanying financial policies.

Constraints

Constraints for sectoral policies are founded in the complexity of socio-economic systems. These do not develop autonomously but are influenced by numerous factors and by actions taken by the public sector. In order to improve living conditions in a region on a long term basis, adaptability and competitiveness must be strengthened. This requires the co-ordinations of industrial policies, labour market policies and educational policies, and maybe even of transportation policies. Any individual sectoral policy on its own will soon reach the limits that arise from a lack of related measures or uncoordinated, counter-productive measures in other fields.

The constraints placed on territorial policies are fundamentally due to the complexity of socio-economic systems. Policies that aim at co-ordinating all measures with territorial impact will only be able to do so for a small territorial unit. The higher up in the hierarchy territorial policy is, the more selectively it must follow a strategic plan and concentrate its goals, planning work and measures on "key areas" that steer development.

The behaviour of the individual political bodies responsible for measures on the different levels depends first on the problem situation and second on their autonomy or independence from others with regard to the measures to be taken.

In Austria, municipalities are endowed with a high degree of formal autonomy and those with financial resources also have the actual power to implement policies. The latter hardly need territorial policies from higher up such as from state government or the federal government. They manage the development process, in part with the help of their own territorial planning strategies. They directly address the competent bodies of the federal government in the field of sectoral policies if they need to. Territorial policies from higher levels are demanded more by disadvantaged areas and municipalities that lack the financial resource and where the aim is to achieve territorial equilibrium.

Austrian states enjoy a high degree of autonomy in keeping with the federalist structure of the country and are also responsible for spatial planning. This planning competence, however, is paired with few powers as far as implementation is concerned since the most important measures concerning infrastructure are the responsibility of the federal government, and zoning is carried out by municipalities. The responsibility for territorial policy is imposed on states by law. However, it is only implemented insofar as it is possible to achieve a consensus with the municipalities on the one hand, and with the federal government on the other hand. Recently demand for territorial "regulation policy" is increasing especially in the field of settlement development. This is due to the scarcity of building land in some reasons and the consequent rise in property prices.

The federal government's competence goes relatively far (e.g. transportation networks and educational facilities) and it has a strong financial policy-making position (its share in public spending is roughly 60 per cent, the remainder is spent by the states and municipalities in equal parts). The federal government also finances the larger part of regional subsidies. However, the task of territorial policy-making is not imposed on it by law and thus it lacks the motivation to overcome the strong resistance of sectoral policies against territorial policy on a national level. Apparently the necessary "problem pressure" is still too low to overcome the dominant sectoral orientation on national level.

The necessary co-ordination with the states and municipalities is usually accomplished along vertical lines within the corresponding fields. This means that, for example, transportation planning by the federal government is co-ordinated with transportation planning by the state -- and thus by - passes a territorial development plan, which exist only partially anyway.

Until recently, the political commitment of the federal government to a territorial orientation has remained limited to certain crisis regions. In these regions it has taken the initiative to start a co-operative effort which includes all political levels (example *Waldviertel*). This type of political initiative would probably be much more difficult to implement on a general state level. As an aside, the necessary co-ordination of sectoral measures with territorial impacts is a task which is not manageable beyond the regional level.

It might be that territorial planning on a national level will receive new stimuli from the supranational level. The increased planning activities of the EU aimed at territorial policies could lead to a situation in which territorial interests have to be articulated more clearly on a national level. Currently, the orientation of the EU's structured funds relevant to territorial development is increasing pressure to co-ordinate activities of the federal government and states.

Experience

Territorial planning in the public mind is plausible only on the local level and maybe on the regional level, which includes daily commuters. Beyond this, the necessity for a territorial policy on a political level is only recognised if the connection between differing developments in one's environment also become perceptible for non-experts.

Political awareness of territorial perspectives is usually achieved:

– if regional developmental disparities reach "absolute limits", for example the collapse of supply basic structures, institutions and services as a consequence of demand leaving a region on the one hand, or as the consequence of strain or if local or regional territorial development is faced with an imminent development turnabout due to an infrastructure or investment project (for "better" or for "worse").

Territorial policy requires on every level:

– that the bodies responsible for sectoral measures be convinced to a high degree that the territorial approach is meaningful;

– it can only be achieved if the bodies responsible for sectoral measures are involved in the process of scheme development, which includes conflicts between partners.

One must take care not to "overburden" any one of the levels. Planning and political decisions on the same level shall be taken on the next higher level based on a territorial policy scheme. Bodies responsible on the higher level are further away from the recipients of their measures and thus have more room for meaningful territorial policy measures with "unequal treatment" (e.g. spatial focuses and priorities).

A sound foundation for territorial policy is thus based on the following components:

– a situation requiring simultaneously concrete projects in an apparently cross-sectoral context which will probably lead to extensive changes;

– a political demand requiring measures that are expressed and declared in territorial terms (i.e. the "areas concern" is stronger than others);

Finland

Economic sectors are powerful in Finland. A strong central administration distributes resources to the State's districts and regions, and the municipalities, and unfortunately there has been little co-ordination at either the central or the regional level. Districts and regions belonging to the different ministries are not coterminous, and this has been an added impediment to co-operation. It has been impossible to co-ordinate activities within municipalities, largely because budget grants have been strictly earmarked by economic sector.

An administration which bases its economic policies along sectoral lines is a major obstacle to rural development. To give just one example, in sparsely populated areas it should be possible to combine service supply at multi-service points but this cannot be done without inter-sectoral co-operation and co-ordination. The development of other rural occupations, too, calls for horizontal co-operation and co-ordination between different sectors.

National budget reductions, combined with other problems due to the recent slump, makes it imperative to use rescues far more efficiently at both the central and the regional levels.

Finland is going through a radical administrative reform which is not limited to rural development. The reform is aimed at greater autonomy and initiative at all administrative levels, but especially at the regional and local levels. This will leave the central administration responsible mainly for fixing general lines of development and monitoring implementation.

The development of rural areas calls for specialisation, in order to enable them to compete successfully. Such specialisation is impossible unless it is supported by the decision-making machinery.

The new regional policy regulations that took effect in January 1994 have made it possible to untangle the web of problems that beset rural policy before that date. They oblige the State regional administration to cooperage with municipalities and with the new regional councils, which directly represent the municipalities. Such co-operation is needed in drafting and implementing regional development programmes. Co-ordination at the central level is the responsibility of the Ministry of the Interior.

Regional development programmes comprise both national and EU programmes. The national programmes include the Development Area Programme, the Structural Change Programme for industrial areas, the Expertise

Centres Programme to promote high technology, the Border Area Programme, the Rural Area Programme and the Archipelago Programme. The EU programmes support the national programmes and run parallel with them in their main objectives. But the EU programmes have a smaller budget than the national programmes and they cover a smaller total area.

The national budget includes Regional Development Funds for programme implementation. The funds are used for occupational development and diversification, development of the infrastructure, public investments and the production of services. Other financial sources are also used for implementing the programmes -- mainly State funds, and funding from municipalities, joint municipal organisations and the private sector.

The use of budgetary grants for regional development is decided independently by each national- and regional-level sector. In recent years this decision-making has been delegated, to a growing extent, from the central administration to the regions. The idea is to use the funds more effectively by co-ordinating their use according to the regions' own programme objectives.

In targeting regional development funds, the general goals and priorities of national regional policy are taken into account together with the priorities of the regions' own programme objectives.

In targeting regional development funds, the general goals and priorities of national regional policy are taken into account together with the priorities of the regions' own programmes. Projects propose by regions are given priority provided they do not clash with the broader programme of national development.

Formal agreements are being used as a tool to ensure the long-term engagement of financing partners in the implementation of the programmes. They are also a good basis for monitoring the use of both national and EU financing. They favour continuity and predictability, and they make it easier to co-ordinate the acquisition and use of resources.

The main purpose of regional development is to reduce unemployment by creating permanent jobs, and by increasing and restructuring production. Other objectives are to enhance know-how, increase the attraction of rural areas as places to live and work in, and to improve the physical operating environment and basic services.

However desirable it is, mere improvement is inadequate. In the face of massive unemployment (20 per cent nationally, considerably higher in most of the remote areas), regional development and restructuring are absolute necessities. Co-operation has got off to a good start and joint responsibility for regional and rural development has been accepted.

Based on the results of the OECD Review of Finland's Rural Development Policy, the Finnish government has set up an inter-sectoral Rural Policy Partnership Group for a term extending from 1 May 1995 to 30 April 1998. The responsibilities of the Partnership Group will be to co-ordinate rural development measures and promote an efficient use of resources allotted to rural areas.

France

The changing countryside

The rural areas, although they have always been subject to gradual change, are currently undergoing a process of rapid evolution. Numerous traditional and hitherto solid bases of rural identity and rural economy are being challenged. The logic of the primary sector economy is no longer dominant and agriculture, the archetypal activity of the countryside, no longer has the same reference value. Mobility of individuals and the increasing similarity of rural and urban lifestyles have also significantly altered the social organisation of the countryside, formally based on micro-communities.

Over the past fifty years, the restructuring of the agricultural sector has led to a sharp decline in the labour force. It has also led to economic diversification, upstream and downstream from agricultural production, although often not directly related to it, and to increased differentiation of territories.

The relative importance of agriculture has thus diminished significantly in our rural areas, where it now frequently accounts for about 10 per cent of the working population.

For this reason, the balance among the various functions of the countryside has become unstable and areas which are particularly sensitive in agricultural terms have been faced with rural decline. In some cases rural areas have been abandoned by entire populations, or face new problems linked to a failure to preserve and maintain the surrounding environment.

In addition, structural adjustment of agriculture to meet market realities gives rise, over a considerable proportion of the territory, to uncertainty as to whether minimum human activity and the environment can be maintained. Thus, in France, one-third of cantons are affected by signs of marked instability resulting from the changes described above and other developments.

Admittedly various measures, socio-structural or otherwise, can speed up or slow down these processes. But the long-standing and continuing restructuring of the sector is likely to accentuate disequilibria in many rural areas.

Rural development policies have therefore to take account of changes in the agricultural, forestry and agro-food sector resulting from modernisation of production and market developments which can affect the rural economy as a whole.

But more generally, the concept of the countryside covers the entire economic, social and associative fabric made up of farming, commerce, crafts, services and SME. It also frequently comprises a quality image of landscape, attractive lifestyle, relaxation and leisure. All this reinforces the need to implement development programmes so as to tackle problems of jobs and activities on a global basis. Action should be both selective as to the territories concerned, and consistent in its implementation. It should draw on the endogenous potential and local realities of some territories, to be defined on a relevant scale, so as to accord with specific local economic conditions.

The territorial approach to sectoral policies

Allowance for rural problems is made via sectoral policies which are no longer monolithic

1. Agricultural policy: the reform of the common agricultural policy bears out the diversity of support measures for farmers and adjustments to such measures for the benefit of small farmers and areas with natural handicaps.

   These adjustments, both past and present, reflect the determination to take account of territorial specificities linked to geographic or economic realities and to adapt general horizontal mechanisms to local conditions.

The development of increasingly marked strategies for product quality (quality seals and designations of origin) also reflects a territorial approach.

2. Forestry policy (forestry and timber processing) is also crucial in maintaining employment in many rural areas. What is more, forests, which in France cover more than a quarter of the country, fulfil three complementary functions: production, protection, recreation.

3. Environmental policy: agriculture and forestry take up most of the national territory and are closely linked to the environmental quality of the countryside, which they have, of course, partly shaped and maintained.

Increasingly widely accepted rules are helping to limit the impact of harmful practices, and to promote the positive effects on the environment and on maintenance of the countryside resulting from these activities. Recognition of the strong social demand is increasingly frequently backed by incentive or compensatory support for environmental purposes.

Apart from agriculture, environmental policy also concerns the preservation and maintenance of all those natural resources that make up an important part of the rural heritage.

4. Tourism policy: the development of rural tourism is playing a growing role in areas where conditions are favourable.

Tourism is frequently used to diversify away from farming as it involves a large number of actors. Rural tourism, which faces overall problems of definition and quality of tourist products, of organising actors, of marketing and of infrastructure creation, has to be integrated in a territorial approach to economic development.

A variety of other sectoral policies are required

The countryside could nevertheless be doomed to underdevelopment unless various other sectoral policies can take account of specific needs so as to guarantee its future as regards:

− maintaining shopping and crafts;

− supporting and creating small and medium enterprises;

– spreading technology (information, communications etc.) and strengthening the participation of rural enterprises and industries in research and innovation programmes;

– providing services;

– providing education and vocational training.

These different sectoral policies have to be adapted to the needs of the most threatened rural economies.

They must contribute to rural development by avoiding conflicting efforts, implying appropriate co-ordination to develop synergies, something that often requires complementarity of action and geographic concentration of financial resources and structural measures.

Coherent programming of measures is thus vital. It relies on partnerships which can only emerge and develop on the appropriate territorial scale.

The methodological approach being developed by the European Union in implementing its structural funds is based on these principles, both through global programmes in underdeveloped regions (objective 1) and rural development programmes (objective 5b).

The latter reflect various parameters, notably the level of overall economic development and sensitivity to changes in agriculture.

A major part of national public support forms a counterpart to these Community arrangements, as reflected by implementation of operational development programmes.

Parallel to the adjustment of agriculture to the market economy, Community policy has evolved in its analysis of rural development and in account taken of environmental concerns, as reflected in practical terms in rural development plans and agro-environmental measures.

Other policies also have to be redesigned

It seems that in a large number of cases major structural policies are still based too much on the number of "customers" and on where they are concentrated. Despite efforts already made to develop territorial approaches, allowance for more dispersed populations, and in some cases the advisability of encouraging such dispersal, as well as consideration of the ecological value of territory traversed in the case of infrastructure, must be given a bigger place in decision-making criteria.

French experience of the territorial approach

Nearly 50 years experience

It is true that in historical terms policy to support the countryside originally focused on structural investment to close the gap with the towns, so that the inhabitants of rural areas, wherever they lived, could benefit from running water, electricity, means of communication, socio-cultural facilities and services comparable in quantity and quality (price) to those available in urban areas.

However, owing to the differing situations of rural areas and trends towards decline in certain parts of the country, policy differentiation gradually emerged along with attempts to identify problem areas on socio-economic rather than purely demographic criteria. With time this helped distinguish rural areas where the situation was on the whole favourable from structurally threatened areas and those with severe development handicaps or in a state of economic crisis.

The zoning of rural areas for the purposes of differentiated territorial policies and more regulation to link economy and territory is already a long established reality in France.

However, this territorial typology has been increasingly recognised by the authorities both in national policy (cf. concerted territorial development programmes and identification of threatened rural areas as reflected in State-region plan contracts as from the end of the 1980s) and in Community policy (cf. rural area development programmes cited above).

Various long-standing instruments bear witness in France to the determination to adopt a territorial approach, notably:

- the creation of regional development companies (around 1955);

- the creation of national parks (as from 1960) and regional nature reserves;

- implementation of rural development plans (as from 1970);

- introduction of the special mountain agriculture allowance (1974);

- the creation of the interministerial rural planning and development fund (1979);

- the creation of the intervention fund for autonomous development of mountainous regions (1985);

- introduction of territorial development premiums, helping to combat rural decline etc.

The promotion of rural development is part of current French territorial planning and development policy. That policy is closely linked to two key principles, namely, shifting State decision-making and action to local agencies of the State in the regions and departments, and considerable decentralisation of powers to local authorities.

The Act of March 1982 on the rights and liberties of the communes, departments, regions and the State, and the Decentralisation Act of January 1983 on the distribution of the powers of the communes, departments, regions and the State have resulted in a major shift of responsibilities and funding to the most appropriate levels and territorial structures.

To mitigate the possible harmful consequences of this dispersal of responsibilities, instruments to guarantee consistency, co-ordination and assessment are needed in order to encourage:

- new forms of territorial organisation, notably through co-operation between local authorities;

- clarification of responsibilities as between territorial authorities;

- adjustment of local taxation;

- equalisation of local resources;

- better distribution of State services;

- maintenance or development of other public and private services by means of concerted action to improve them and make them operate effectively on a multi-purpose basis;

- promotion of an agricultural policy whereby occupancy of rural land is recognised as a vocation complementary to that of producing foodstuffs;

- exploitation of natural amenities, notably through tourism;

- diversification of economic activity, and incentives to the creation of industry and services in rural areas.

Recent trends

In the legislative field, advances of various kinds reflect concern with the local development approach. The Act of February 1992 on administration of the national territory, which encourages links between local authorities, as well as direct taxation and extended responsibilities, is going to mean more territorial projects and illustrates the increasing use made of the concept of development on an appropriate territorial basis.

The general Act on territorial planning and development recently adopted by the French Parliament reinforces the allowance made for territorial approaches. Territorial development directives will reflect the broad lines laid down in the national plan, just as regional territorial planning and development plans will set out, for each region, the main development issues and the general policy advocated.

Definition of rural areas of special interest will, without eliminating existing administrative territorial sub-divisions, give recognition to specific country lifestyles and communities of economic and social interests, and will offer a framework for adapting the way services are organised, as well as for various partnerships for common development and intercommunal projects. This concept of "special rural areas", which emerged in the 1970s and is still relevant today, is thus now acquiring a new significance.

Imbalances will be corrected:

- firstly, by redefining priority development areas where the State and local authorities can apply exceptional or concessionary fiscal or social regimes for the benefit of enterprises or individuals, providing for two levels of incentives: priority rural development areas (some 12 million inhabitants) and rural revitalisation areas, a sub-group in the most remote parts of the country (some 4 million inhabitants);

- secondly, through a policy of equal access to services to limit the effects of closures of services provided by public establishments and national enterprises, and to stimulate the development of multi-purpose services.

Continuing decentralisation will be backed by:

- updating the equalisation of resources of local authorities, through reform of local taxation and finances, and by means of a redistributive mechanism to improve the sharing of available resources, having regard to the outgoing and income of local authorities;

- clarification of responsibilities between levels of territorial authorities.

Territorial organisation and management of rural areas thus imply concern for a more balanced and more harmonious distribution of activities and population, and integration of activities -- economic or otherwise -- in a global approach adapted to project development, including projects shared between towns and countryside. This approach demonstrates the inadequacies of dealing with economic sectors separately; it addresses human and social aspects, and integrates heritage-based considerations.

The rural world, which feels excluded from matters of concern at national level, is coming to be included among the major choices affecting the future of the national territory, as a result of a territorial development policy which bridges the divisions that separate sectoral responsibilities.

Main ways of deepening the territorial approach

These involve:

– increasing and diversifying approaches, instruments and procedures applied;

– examining how development arrangements of increasing complexity can fit together. Possible confusion can be avoided by interlinking the growing mass of data and parameters and processing them in a co-ordinated fashion. The aim is to deal globally with sectoral problems and concerns relating to housing, tourism, the environment, rural development, agriculture and economic diversification;

– commitment by the population and their mobilisation as actors in a collective territorial development project. The growing complexity of action to be undertaken is however a matter for experts. This problem has to be addressed by local elected representatives, who are required to integrate and arbitrate between individual interests, and to explain development projects to the citizens of the territories and areas concerned;

– education in local development to ensure that voluntary associations and occupational groups collaborate fully;

– appropriate institutional arrangements and the setting up of advisory committees;

– mitigating the negative effects of self-centred projects, which can lead to dynamic regions becoming richer and disadvantaged ones becoming poorer, by applying compensatory and solidarity mechanisms (zoning, equalisation of capital and operating grants).

Thus in France, preparation and implementation of State-region plan contracts, which are five-year planning documents for joint funding by the State and the region of jointly defined priority objectives, have to include assessment of the ability of territorial structures to implement projects.

The single programming documents for action by the European Union in the rural development field (objective 5b and LEADER initiative programme) which integrate and co-ordinate financial intervention by macro-territorial levels, also need to be backed by local rural development strategies.

Conclusion

Rural development, which aims to spread the effects of economic, social and cultural growth throughout the countryside, requires an understanding of economic impacts and redistribution mechanisms. If it is to be lasting it has to integrate environmental concerns in all development projects and satisfy present needs without compromising the future. This calls for an integrated approach, including training aspects and innovation requirements in rural areas, whereby questions arising in any territory which affirms its determination to develop are addressed in global terms.

PART III   RURAL DEVELOPMENT IN FIGURES

RURAL EMPLOYMENT INDICATORS

The OECD Rural Development Programme was launched in 1991 with the aim of analysing opportunities and options for rural development. A central part of this Programme is its Activity on Rural Indicators. It aims to create a quantified territorial information base facilitating international comparison and co-operation on rural development and rural policies in OECD Member countries.

The Activity on Rural Indicators has:

– established a *territorial scheme* for collecting and providing statistics on sub-national territorial units in a multi-national context;

– selected a *basic set of rural indicators* addressing demographic, economic, social and environmental concerns;

– produced a *first series of statistics* for empirical analysis of rural development conditions and trends in OECD.

Thus far, work on rural indicators focused in particular on rural employment issues, in accordance with the priorities of the Rural Development Programme. Future work will also concentrate on improving the information base concerning the social and environmental dimensions of rural development.

Territorial scheme for OECD Analysis

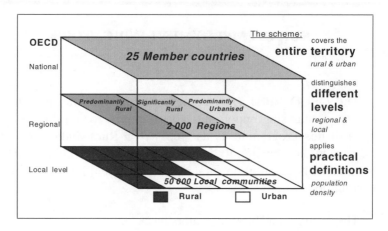

Source: OECD Rural Data Surveys.

The territorial scheme for empirical analysis of territorial development conditions and trends in OECD covers the entire territory of the 25 OECD Member countries, not just rural areas.

The distinction of different hierarchical levels for territorial analysis is crucial in understanding the conceptual approach of the OECD work on rural indicators:

− at the local level, the territorial grid consists of basic administrative or statistical units that can be classified as being either rural or urban;

− at the regional level, larger administrative or functional areas like provinces, commuting zones etc. can be characterised as being more or less rural.

To identify rural communities at the local level OECD uses a simple and intuitive criterion: population density. At the more aggregate level, regions are grouped according to their degree of rurality (regional share of rural population).

Rural population and area -- their importance

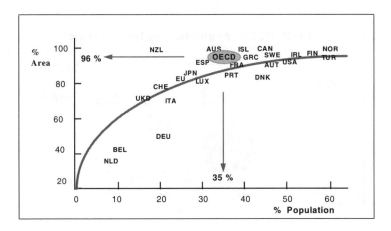

Source: OECD Rural Data Surveys.

At the local level OECD identifies rural areas as communities with low population density. According to this definition,

National shares of populations living in rural communities range from less than 10 per cent, in the Netherlands and Belgium, to over 50 per cent in parts of Scandinavia and in Turkey.

This does not mean that rural development issues are less important in some countries than in others. However, rural problems and perspectives, and hence rural policy issues and approaches will often be different.

Rural typology -- three types of region

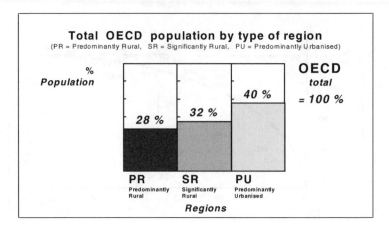

Source: OECD Rural Data Surveys.

Development options and opportunities for local rural communities, to a large degree, depend on their relationship with urban centres, in particular those within their own region.

For analytical purposes the 2 000 OECD regions can be grouped into three types, which are defined by the share of population living in rural communities:

- *predominantly rural regions* are those with over 50 per cent of the population being rural;

- *significantly rural regions* are those with 15 to 50 per cent;

- *predominantly urbanised regions* are those with less than 15 per cent of rural population.

Thus each of the three types of region contain some rural and some urban communities although to a differing degree.

In total, about a quarter (28%) of the OECD population dwell in predominantly rural, often remote regions with a majority of people in sparsely populated, rural communities. At the other extreme, about 40 per cent of the OECD population is concentrated on less than 3 per cent of the territory in predominantly urbanised regions. The remaining third of the population (32%) lives in the intermediate category of significantly rural regions.

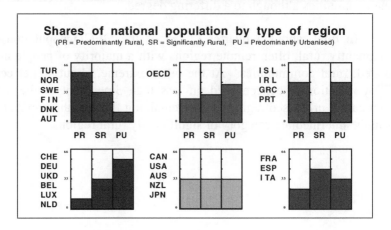

Source: OECD Rural Data Surveys.

The spatial organisation of OECD Member countries is characterised by a great diversity of territorial patterns. The distribution of national populations over the three types of region differs a lot.

In some countries (Turkey, Scandinavia, Austria) population shares descend from predominantly rural regions (PR), to significantly rural (SR), to predominantly urbanised regions (PU), while in others population shares ascend (BENELUX-countries, United Kingdom, Germany and Switzerland).

Some countries are characterised by a dual structure with large proportions of the population at both extremes, predominantly rural and predominantly urbanised (Iceland, Ireland, Greece and Portugal), while in France, Spain and Italy the largest share is in the intermediate, significantly rural regions.

Lastly, other Member countries are, on the whole, characterised by a less accentuated distribution of their population, showing almost equal shares in all three types of region.

This simple comparison already reveals common characteristics shared by different Member countries which serve to facilitate a better understanding of their perceptions and their relative policy approaches to rural development.

100

Rural Indicators -- a basic set

POPULATION AND MIGRATION	SOCIAL WELL-BEING AND EQUITY
Density Change Structure Households Communities	Income Housing Education Health Safety
ECONOMIC STRUCTURE AND PERFORMANCE	ENVIRONMENT AND SUSTAINABILITY
Labour force Employment Sectoral shares Productivity Investment	Topography and Climate Land use change Habitats and Species Soils and Water Air quality

Source: OECD Rural Data Surveys.

Rural Development is a complex, multi-sectoral concept. Thus rural conditions and trends can only be described by using a comprehensive set of rural indicators. OECD's basic set of rural indicators addresses four main rural development concerns: demographic, economic, social, and environmental.

For more detailed rural analyses, specific territorial statistics, for example on commuting, enterprise structure, educational levels, rural tourism or on agricultural structures, shall be gathered using the same territorial scheme. They complete and complement the information contained in the basic indicator set.

Rural employment -- sectoral shares

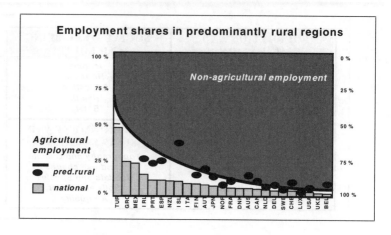

Source: OECD Rural Data Surveys.

Work on rural employment has been a top priority for the OECD Rural Development Programme.

For a long time agriculture was considered the most important economic activity in rural areas. This is no longer true. Thus, rural employment should not be confused with employment in agriculture. The share of the agricultural sector -- including fisheries and forestry -- in the total national employment ranges from over 20 per cent in Turkey, Greece and Mexico to less than 5 per cent in Belgium, Luxembourg, the United Kingdom, United States, Switzerland, Sweden and Germany.

Of course, in all countries the share of agricultural employment is higher in rural regions than elsewhere. But even in predominantly rural regions, the share of agricultural employment is below 25 per cent in most OECD Member countries.

This means that the vast majority of rural employment opportunities is in non-agricultural employment. Today, also rural people are mainly engaged in manufacturing and service activities.

Rural employment -- change

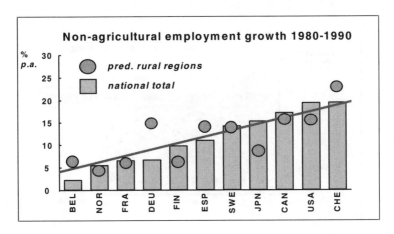

Non-agricultural employment growth 1980-1990

Source: OECD Rural Data Surveys.

The opportunities for rural employment creation are often better than usually expected. While agricultural employment is decreasing, rural employment is increasing in most parts of OECD.

On average, during the eighties, even the predominantly rural regions experienced growth in non-agricultural employment. In many countries, however, the rural increase did not keep pace with the national rate of employment creation.

Conversely, some countries, in particular those with comparatively few predominantly rural regions, such as Switzerland, Germany and Belgium, have experienced growth in non-agricultural rural employment higher than the national average.

Employment Change -- by region 1980-1990 (Austria)

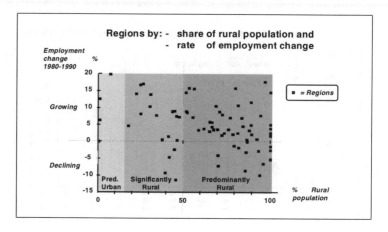

Source: OECD Rural Data Surveys.

If employment change is analysed in a territorially disaggregated manner, like in the above graph, using Austria as a clear but not untypical example, it becomes evident that there is a wide range of development options and opportunities even for the most rural regions.

In the graph, all the Austrian regions are plotted according to both their degree of rurality (share of rural population), and their rate of total employment change (1980 to 1990). Consequently, regions cannot only be grouped into predominantly, or significantly rural, and predominantly urbanised regions, but also into growing (or dynamic) and declining (or lagging) regions.

The fact that regions can have the same degree of rurality but perform very differently should have implications for the design of rural analyses and rural policies. In addition to comparing rural with urban, the focus should be on the comparative (dis)advantages among the rural regions. By analysing and better understanding the diversity of development potentials and policy contexts that make some rural territories more successful than others, it should become possible *to design better rural policies*.

This will require broadening the scope of OECD analyses from a sectoral and time series oriented perspective to a territorially differentiated approach, enabling better horizontal integration of the demographic, economic, social and environmental dimensions of development, as well as providing a basis for improved co-operation between local, regional, national and international levels of administration.

ANNEXES

ANNEX I   BACKGROUND DOCUMENTS FOR THE HIGH-LEVEL MEETING

1. Publications by the Rural Development Programme (1991 to present)

What Future for Our Countryside?   A Rural Development Policy (OECD, 1993)

This is the reference document for rural development policy in the context of OECD.   After an analysis of rural problems and potentials, it proposes a development policy formulated around clearly defined objectives. The objectives cover the economic, social, and environmental realm and the proposed responses are two-tiered: a general set of measures for all rural areas and specific measures targeted to three types of rural areas.   The report takes a territorial approach -- as opposed to a sectoral one -- to tackle the horizontal nature of rural development policy.

Creating Rural Indicators for Shaping Territorial Policy (OECD, 1994)

This publication provides a quantitative back-up to *What Future for our countryside?   A Rural Development Policy* and opens the way to the internationally harmonised processing of statistics collected for sub-national territorial entities.   After a discussion of the theoretical concept, a geographical scheme is proposed and lastly, tables are given setting out a number of key indicators for rural development, highlighting territorial differences for three types of regions.

The Contribution of Amenities to Rural Development (OECD, 1994)

This publication highlights the different elements of the natural and man-made heritage -- also called amenities -- found in rural areas.   After an analysis of the economic characteristics of rural amenities, it explores policy mechanisms by which the values society increasingly puts on such amenities can be better captured by those who provide them, thus enhancing the economic development opportunities for rural areas.

Niche Goods and Services for a Rural Development Strategy (OECD, 1995)

This publication shows how niche marketing -- a specific form of commercialisation -- can foster rural development. In light of the growing demand for goods and services linked to natural resources or cultural identity, rural businesses have emerging opportunities to exploit their comparative advantage in many innovative ways. The basic prerequisite for developing niche markets are examined, opening the door to policy requirements.

Government Measures for Rural Employment Creation (OECD, 1995)

This report discusses the effectiveness of employment promotion programmes in rural areas and their contribution to rural development. After framing rural employment creation in the context of the OECD work on employment, the report addresses four critical policy areas for rural development: direct aid, indirect aid, enhancement of human resources, and infrastructure programmes. Finally, principles for an innovative strategy to foster rural employment are laid out, taking into account the major differences among the three types of rural areas.

Review of National Rural Policy: Finland (OECD, 1995) and Switzerland (OECD, GD, 1995)

Reviewing rural policy in individual Member countries was undertaken for the first time in 1994. These reviews are aimed at both helping the candidates in their efforts to strengthen rural policy and providing other Member countries with an in-depth analysis of rural issues and policies. The framework *What Future for Our Countryside? A Rural Development Policy* was used for both reviews. The nature of the review, however, was different for Finland and Switzerland, as the former addressed a policy already in place, while the latter examined a proposal for a new programme.

2. Reports by the Rural Development Unit of the OECD Public Management Service (1988 - 1991)

New Trends in Rural Policy Making (OECD, 1988)

This book reviews the trends in the development and in the management systems of the rural economy. It stresses the importance of the territorial approach, of the responsibility of the new actors, of institutional mechanisms and procedures, and of decentralisation for rural development. The second part of the book is reserved for a country analysis of the management processes of rural policies in 16 Member countries.

Partnerships for Rural Development (OECD, 1990)

This report reviews the organisational and policy aspects that underpin effective partnership machinery, describes examples of different institutional partnerships and assesses their prospects for successful implementation of rural development programmes. In many OECD countries, new kinds of institutional partnerships are being formed to implement integrated rural development policies. Partnerships that include different levels of government, business, voluntary organisations and elected officials have proved an effective response to an increasingly diversified rural economy.

New Ways of Managing Services in Rural Areas (OECD, 1991)

This survey describes new strategies being implemented in OECD countries to facilitate the emergence of services specifically suited to the new demands of rural areas. Services -- schools, communications, health and commercial facilities -- are an integral part of the economic, social and cultural life of rural areas. Their accessibility and quality are a significant factor in the development of the countryside.

3. Publications by Other OECD Bodies

Tourism Strategies and Rural Development (OECD/GD(94)49)

This report was prepared by the Tourism Committee in collaboration with the Rural Development Programme. It studies the relationships between the growth of the tourism sector and the development of rural areas, notably what are the distinguishing characteristics of rural tourism, what is its development potential in various types of rural areas, and how can it generate employment and attract capital to such areas. The role of the various levels of governments and the private sector to harnessing tourism potential in rural areas is also discussed.

Farm Employment and Economic Adjustment in OECD Countries (OECD, 1994)

This report, prepared by the Committee of Agriculture, examines the pressures and opportunities that farmers in OECD Member countries could face following the reform of agricultural policies. Although the most significant impacts on employment in the agricultural sectors are likely to stem from long-term demographic factors, the greatest job losses due to policy reform may well occur in the sectors upstream and downstream from agriculture. Nonetheless, an integrated and well targeted policy approach can play a role in facilitating the adjustment process by focusing on improving factor mobility. Towards this end, a policy framework which includes social, educational and infrastructural policies and programmes should aim to strengthen the long-term viability of the agricultural sector as a whole.

Territorial Development and Structural Change (OECD, 1993)

This report by the Co-operative Action Programme on Local Economic and Employment Development takes stock of the influence and relevance of local development efforts in the context of constant structural adjustment and high and lasting unemployment. It seeks to discuss, on the basis on concrete examples, the role and responsibilities of government in fostering development, and to establish some guidelines for action.

Women and Structural Change -- New Perspectives (OECD, 1994)

The first part of this publication examines the relationship between structural adjustment and the integration of women into OECD economies in the 1990s and identifies directions for action related to family and employment, occupational segregation and employment flexibility. The second part, a technical report, provides an analysis of the impact of structural change on women's employment, especially the growth in part-time work, and trends in the service and public sectors. It considers the efficacy of existing equal employment opportunity policies in a constantly changing environment.

Globalisation and Local and Regional Competitiveness (OECD/GD(94)13)

This study was prepared by the Working Party No. 6 on Regional Policies. It aims to analyse the impact of the increasing globalisation of industrial and service activities on the conditions of regional and local competitiveness, and to assess its policy implications at various levels of government, both for developed and lagging regions.

ANNEX II   LIST OF PARTICIPANTS

PRESIDENT

Ms. Gunhild ØYANGEN

Minister of Agriculture of Norway

OPENING SPEECH

M. Jean-Claude PAYE

Secretary-General

CHAIRMAN OF THE GROUP OF THE COUNCIL ON RURAL DEVELOPMENT

Mr. Richard W. LONG

SESSION I RURAL DEVELOPMENT: LESSONS AND CHALLENGES

Mr. Kenneth L. DEAVERS

Chairman of the Group of the Council on Rural Development

from 1990 to 1994

High-Level Meeting
of the Group of the Council on Rural Development
10-11 April 1995

AUSTRALIA

Mr. Onko KINGMA — Assistant Secretary, Department of Primary Industries and Energy

Mr. Philip HARRINGTON — Minister, Permanent Delegation

AUSTRIA

Mr. Dkfm. Ulrich STACHER — Director General for Economic Co-ordination
Federal Chancellery

Mr. Prof. POSCHACHER — Deputy Director General, Ministry for Agriculture and Forestry

Mr. Thomas DAX — Federal Institute for Less Favoured and Mountainous Areas

Mr. Roland ARBTER — Federal Chancellery

Mr. Rudolf NIESSLER — Conseiller, Permanent Delegation

BELGIUM

M. C. CROHAIN — Secrétaire Général, Ministère de l'Agriculture

M. Emile DETRAUX — Directeur du Service des Relations Internationales Agricoles, Ministère de l'Agriculture

M. Jacques REGINSTER — Administrateur Général, Office Wallon de Développement Rural

M. Georges CHRISTOPHE — Président,Fondation Rurale de Wallonie

M. Marc QUOIDBACH — Attaché, Fondation Rurale de Wallonie

Mlle. Carine PETIT — Premier Secrétaire, Délégation Permanente

Mr. Pierre LAMBOTTE — Conseiller, Délégation Permanente

CANADA

Mr. John R. McWHINNIE — Director General, Labour Market Services, Human Resources Development

Mr. Dennis G. STEPHENS — Special Advisor, Rural Renewal, Agriculture and Agri-Food Canada

Ms. Heather CLEMENSON — Rural Renewal, Agriculture and Agri-Food Canada

Mr. Peter McGOVERN — First Secretary, Permanent Delegation

DENMARK

Mr. Henrik Torp ANDERSEN — Head of Section , Ministry of the Interior

Ms. Inga Steen JENSEN — Head of Division, Ministry of Agriculture and Fisheries

Mr. Ture FALBE-HANSEN — Secrétaire d'Ambassade, Permanent Delegation

FINLAND

Mr. Jikka RUSKA — Director General, Ministry of Agriculture and Forestry

Mr. Paavo PIRTTIMÄKI — Director General, Ministry of the Interior

Mr Ilkka VAINIO-MATTILA — Director General, Ministry of Agriculture and Forestry

Mr. Kari GRÖHN — Special Advisor, Rural Policy Committee, Ministry of the Interior

Mr. Antero TUOMINEN — Conseiller, Permanent Delegation

FRANCE	M. André GRAMMONT	Directeur de l'Espace Rural et de la Forêt, Ministère de l'Agriculture
	M. Jean-Louis GUIGOU	Directeur de la DATAR, Ministère de l'Interieur et de l'Aménagement du Territoire
	Mme Christine KOVACSHAZY	Chargée des Affaires Rurales, Commissariat Général du Plan
	M. Denis BAVARD	Sous-directeur du Développement Rural, Ministère de l'Agriculture
	M. Michel LEGRAS	Conseiller, Délégation Permanente
GERMANY	Mr. Reinhard SCHIFFNER	Director, Federal Ministry of Food, Agriculture and Forestry
	Mr. Theo AUGUSTIN	Federal Ministry of Food, Agriculture and Forestry
	Mr. Heinz-Ditmar SCHRAMM	Second Secretary, Permanent Delegation
GREECE	Mme Kalliopi PACHAKI	Scientific Researcher, Centre of Planning and Economic Research (KEPE)
	Mr. Panayotis KOUTSOUVELIS	Deputy Permanent Representative, Permanent Delegation
	Mme. Tarsia MARKOMICHELAKI	Conseiller, Permanent Delegation
IRELAND	Mr. John FOX	Rural Development Division, Department of Agriculture, Food and Forestry
	Mr. Michael CRONIN	First Secretary, Permanent Delegation
ITALY	Prof. Corrado BARBERIS	Président de l'Institut de Sociologie Rurale
	M. Paolo MENNUNI	Dép. pour la Co-ordination des politiques communautaires, Présidence du Conseil des Ministres
	Dr. Mario AMBROGETTI	Directeur général, Ministère du Budget et de la Programmation Economique
	Dr. Egidio SARDO	Fonctionnaire Agricole, Ministère des Ressources Agricoles, Alimentaires et Forestières
	M. Ciro IMPAGNATIELLO	Fonctionnaire Agricole, Ministère des Ressources Agricoles, Alimentaires et Forestières
	M. Ernesto BATTISTI	Attaché, Délégation Permanente
JAPAN	Mr. Toshinori KIKUCHI	Director General, Planning Department, Agricultural Structure Improvement Bureau, Ministry of Agriculture, Forestry and Fisheries
	Mr. Yasuo NAMIKAWA	Deputy Director, Regional Planning Division, Agricultural Structure Improvement Bureau, Ministry of Agriculture, Forestry and Fisheries
	Mr. Masahito HATOYAMA	Deputy Director, Regional Planning Division, Agricultural Structure Improvement Bureau, Ministry of Agriculture, Forestry and Fisheries

JAPAN (continued)	Mr. Shigenobu OGURA	Chief, Rural Employment Improvement Division, Agricultural Structure Improvement Bureau, Ministry of Agriculture, Forestry and Fisheries
	Mr. Syuji YAMADA	Counsellor, Permanent Delegation
	Mr. Makoto OSAWA	First Secretary, Permanent Delegation
LUXEMBURG	M. Jean-Pierre DICHTER	Premier Conseiller du Gouvernement, Ministère de l'Agriculture, de la Viticulture et du Développement Rural
MEXICO	Ms. Adriana MAÍZ	Assistant Deputy Secretary for Economic and Social Analysis, Ministry of Social Development
	Mr. Daniel DULTZIN	Ambassador, Permanent Delegation
NEW-ZEALAND	Ms. Pamela WILKINSON	First Secretary, Permanent Delegation
NETHERLANDS	Mr. Johan F. de LEEUW	Director General, Ministry of Agriculture, Nature Management and Fisheries
	Mr. Albert J. VERMUE	Staff Officer International Affairs, Ministry of Agriculture, Nature Mannagement and Fisheries
	Mr. Dick E. OELE	Manager, Rural Development Programmes, Ministry of Agriculture, Nature Management and Fisheries
	Ms. Riemke JAANUS	Agricultural Attaché, Royal Dutch Embassy
	Mr. Jaap J. PAPE	Agricultural Councillor, Royal Dutch Embassy
NORWAY	Mrs. Oddny BANG	State Secretary, Ministry of Local Government and Labour
	Mr. Ottar BEFRING	State Secretary, Ministry of Agriculture
	Mr. Jan SANDAL	Director General, Ministry of Local Government and Labour
	Mr. Per OFSTAD	Deputy Director General, Ministry of Agriculture
	Mrs. Kirsten AGERUP	Project Manager, Ministry of Local Government and Labour
	Mr. Per M. ØLBERG	Ambassador, Permanent Delegation
	Mr. Ola STORENG	Special Counsellor, Permanent Delegation
PORTUGAL	M. Romeu REIS	Counsellor, Secretariat of State for Regional Development
	M. Carlos COSTA	Vice-Président, Institut de Structures Agraires et Développement Rural, Ministère de l'Agriculture
	Dr. Vitor SANTOS	Directeur des Services, Direction Générale du Développement Regional, Ministère du Plan et de l'Administration du Territoire
	M. António Lourenço dos SANTOS	Conseiller, Délégation Permanente

SPAIN	M. José Luis GOMEZ GIL	Sous-directeur Général des Affaires Communautaires, Ministère de l'Agriculture, de la Pêche et de l'Alimentation
	M. Roberto SANCHO HAZAK	Chef de Planification, Secrétariat Général des Structures Agraires, Ministère de l'Agriculture, de la Pêche et de l'Alimentation
	Mme. Pilar GARCÉS MONTERO	Directeur des Programmes, Direction Générale d'Action Economiques Territoriales, Ministère de l'Administration Publique
	M. Jesus GONZALES REGIDOR	Conseiller, Délégation Permanente
SWEDEN	Mr. Erling KRISTIANSSON	Head of Section, Ministry of Labour
	Ms. Karin ALM	Head of Section, Ministry of Labour
	Ms. Maria GUSTAVSSON	Director, National Rural Area Development Agency
	Ms. Annika MOLIN HELLGREN	Second Secretary, Permanent Delegation
SWITZERLAND	M. Simon HUBER	Chef, Centrale pour le développement économique régional, Office fédéral de l'industrie, des arts et métiers et du travail
	M. Rudolf SCHIESS	Chef, Section Questions de planification, Office Fédéral de l'industrie, des arts et métiers et du travail
	Mr. Thomas MAIER	Division Principale, Paiements directs et structure, Office Fédéral de l'Agriculture
	M. Rodolfo LAUB	Conseiller d'Ambassade, Délégation Permanente
TURKEY	Dr. Orhan GUVENEN	Ambassadeur, Permanent Delegation
	Mr. Erkan BENLI	Agriculture Counsellor, Permanent Delegation
UNITED KINGDOM	Ms. Bryony HOULDEN	Rural Development Division, Department of the Environment
	Mr. John TAYLOR	Deputy Chief Executive and Director of Operations, Rural Development Commission
	Mr. David WALWYN	Economic Secretary, Permanent Delegation
UNITED STATES	Mr. John DUNMORE	Acting Administrator, Economic Research Service, U.S. Department of Agriculture
	Ms. Sara MAZIE	Acting Associate Administrator, Economic Research Service, U.S. Department of Agriculture
	Mr. Philip WALL	Advisor, Permanent Delegation
COMMISSION OF THE EUROPEAN COMMUNITIES	M. Laurent van DEPOELE	Directeur, Agriculture and Rural Development, D.G. VI
	M. Ferdinand DUSAUSOY	Principal Administrator, Agriculture and Rural Development, D.G. VI

Observers

COUNCIL OF EUROPE	Mr. Halvor LERVIK	Secretary, Committee on Agriculture and Rural Development
	Ms. Graziella BRIANZONI	Head of Paris Office
F.A.O.	Ms. Tea PETRIN	Rural Development Officer
BUSINESS AND INDUSTRY ADVISORY COMMITTEE TO THE OECD (BIAC)	Mr. Giannino C. BERNABEI	Conseiller au Comité Economique et Social de l'UE
TRADE UNION ADVISORY COMMITTEE TO THE OECD (TUAC)	Mr. John EVANS	General Secretary TUAC
	Mr. Andreas BOTSCH	Assistant
	Mr. Mike LESCAULT	Deputy Representative, American Federation of Labor and Congress of Industrial Organizations (AFL-CIO)
POLAND	Mr. Benicjuscz KRAMSKI	Directeur Adjoint, Département des Sciences, Education et Techniques, Ministère de l'Agriculture et de l'Economie Alimentaire

Secretariat

OECD SECRETARIAT	M. Jean-Claude PAYE	Secretary General
	M. Pierre VINDE	Deputy Secretary General
TERRITORIAL DEVELOPMENT SERVICE	M. Christopher BROOKS	Head of Service
RURAL DEVELOPMENT PROGRAMME	M. Gösta OSCARSSON	Head
	M. Christian HUILLET	Deputy Head
	M. Kenji YOSHINAGA	Administrator
	M. Philippe MUHEIM	Administrator
	M. Heino von MEYER	Consultant
	M. David FRESHWATER	Consultant
AGRICULTURE DIVISION	M. Gérard VIATTE	Director

MAIN SALES OUTLETS OF OECD PUBLICATIONS
PRINCIPAUX POINTS DE VENTE DES PUBLICATIONS DE L'OCDE

ARGENTINA – ARGENTINE
Carlos Hirsch S.R.L.
Galería Güemes, Florida 165, 4° Piso
1333 Buenos Aires   Tel. (1) 331.1787 y 331.2391
                         Telefax: (1) 331.1787

AUSTRALIA – AUSTRALIE
D.A. Information Services
648 Whitehorse Road, P.O.B 163
Mitcham, Victoria 3132   Tel. (03) 9210.7777
                             Telefax: (03) 9210.7788

AUSTRIA – AUTRICHE
Gerold & Co.
Graben 31
Wien I   Tel. (0222) 533.50.14
                         Telefax: (0222) 512.47.31.29

BELGIUM – BELGIQUE
Jean De Lannoy
Avenue du Roi 202 Koningslaan
B-1060 Bruxelles   Tel. (02) 538.51.69/538.08.41
                        Telefax: (02) 538.08.41

CANADA
Renouf Publishing Company Ltd.
1294 Algoma Road
Ottawa, ON K1B 3W8   Tel. (613) 741.4333
                          Telefax: (613) 741.5439
Stores:
61 Sparks Street
Ottawa, ON K1P 5R1   Tel. (613) 238.8985
12 Adelaide Street West
Toronto, ON M5H 1L6   Tel. (416) 363.3171
                          Telefax: (416)363.59.63

Les Éditions La Liberté Inc.
3020 Chemin Sainte-Foy
Sainte-Foy, PQ G1X 3V6   Tel. (418) 658.3763
                              Telefax: (418) 658.3763

Federal Publications Inc.
165 University Avenue, Suite 701
Toronto, ON M5H 3B8   Tel. (416) 860.1611
                           Telefax: (416) 860.1608

Les Publications Fédérales
1185 Université
Montréal, QC H3B 3A7   Tel. (514) 954.1633
                            Telefax: (514) 954.1635

CHINA – CHINE
China National Publications Import
Export Corporation (CNPIEC)
16 Gongti E. Road, Chaoyang District
P.O. Box 88 or 50
Beijing 100704 PR   Tel. (01) 506.6688
                         Telefax: (01) 506.3101

CHINESE TAIPEI – TAIPEI CHINOIS
Good Faith Worldwide Int'l. Co. Ltd.
9th Floor, No. 118, Sec. 2
Chung Hsiao E. Road
Taipei   Tel. (02) 391.7396/391.7397
              Telefax: (02) 394.9176

**CZECH REPUBLIC –
RÉPUBLIQUE TCHÈQUE**
Artia Pegas Press Ltd.
Narodni Trida 25
POB 825
111 21 Praha 1   Tel. (2) 242 246 04
                      Telefax: (2) 242 278 72

DENMARK – DANEMARK
Munksgaard Book and Subscription Service
35, Nørre Søgade, P.O. Box 2148
DK-1016 København K   Tel. (33) 12.85.70
                           Telefax: (33) 12.93.87

EGYPT – ÉGYPTE
Middle East Observer
41 Sherif Street
Cairo   Tel. 392.6919
                        Telefax: 360-6804

FINLAND – FINLANDE
Akateeminen Kirjakauppa
Keskuskatu 1, P.O. Box 128
00100 Helsinki
Subscription Services/Agence d'abonnements :
P.O. Box 23
00371 Helsinki   Tel. (358 0) 121 4416
                      Telefax: (358 0) 121.4450

FRANCE
OECD/OCDE
Mail Orders/Commandes par correspondance :
2, rue André-Pascal
75775 Paris Cedex 16   Tel. (33-1) 45.24.82.00
                           Telefax: (33-1) 49.10.42.76
                           Telex: 640048 OCDE
Internet: Compte.PUBSINQ @ oecd.org

Orders via Minitel, France only/
Commandes par Minitel, France exclusivement :
36 15 OCDE

OECD Bookshop/Librairie de l'OCDE :
33, rue Octave-Feuillet
75016 Paris   Tel. (33-1) 45.24.81.81
                   (33-1) 45.24.81.67

Dawson
B.P. 40
91121 Palaiseau Cedex   Tel. 69.10.47.00
                             Telefax : 64.54.83.26

Documentation Française
29, quai Voltaire
75007 Paris   Tel. 40.15.70.00

Economica
49, rue Héricart
75015 Paris   Tel. 45.78.12.92
                   Telefax : 40.58.15.70

Gibert Jeune (Droit-Économie)
6, place Saint-Michel
75006 Paris   Tel. 43.25.91.19

Librairie du Commerce International
10, avenue d'Iéna
75016 Paris   Tel. 40.73.34.60

Librairie Dunod
Université Paris-Dauphine
Place du Maréchal-de-Lattre-de-Tassigny
75016 Paris   Tel. 44.05.40.13

Librairie Lavoisier
11, rue Lavoisier
75008 Paris   Tel. 42.65.39.95

Librairie des Sciences Politiques
30, rue Saint-Guillaume
75007 Paris   Tel. 45.48.36.02

P.U.F.
49, boulevard Saint-Michel
75005 Paris   Tel. 43.25.83.40

Librairie de l'Université
12a, rue Nazareth
13100 Aix-en-Provence   Tel. (16) 42.26.18.08

Documentation Française
165, rue Garibaldi
69003 Lyon   Tel. (16) 78.63.32.23

Librairie Decitre
29, place Bellecour
69002 Lyon   Tel. (16) 72.40.54.54

Librairie Sauramps
Le Triangle
34967 Montpellier Cedex 2   Tel. (16) 67.58.85.15
                                 Tekefax: (16) 67.58.27.36

A la Sorbonne Actual
23, rue de l'Hôtel-des-Postes
06000 Nice   Tel. (16) 93.13.77.75
                  Telefax: (16) 93.80.75.69

GERMANY – ALLEMAGNE
OECD Publications and Information Centre
August-Bebel-Allee 6
D-53175 Bonn   Tel. (0228) 959.120
                    Telefax: (0228) 959.12.17

GREECE – GRÈCE
Librairie Kauffmann
Mavrokordatou 9
106 78 Athens   Tel. (01) 32.55.321
                     Telefax: (01) 32.30.320

HONG-KONG
Swindon Book Co. Ltd.
Astoria Bldg. 3F
34 Ashley Road, Tsimshatsui
Kowloon, Hong Kong   Tel. 2376.2062
                          Telefax: 2376.0685

HUNGARY – HONGRIE
Euro Info Service
Margitsziget, Európa Ház
1138 Budapest   Tel. (1) 111.62.16
                     Telefax: (1) 111.60.61

ICELAND – ISLANDE
Mál Mog Menning
Laugavegi 18, Pósthólf 392
121 Reykjavik   Tel. (1) 552.4240
                     Telefax: (1) 562.3523

INDIA – INDE
Oxford Book and Stationery Co.
Scindia House
New Delhi 110001   Tel. (11) 331.5896/5308
                        Telefax: (11) 332.5993
17 Park Street
Calcutta 700016   Tel. 240832

INDONESIA – INDONÉSIE
Pdii-Lipi
P.O. Box 4298
Jakarta 12042   Tel. (21) 573.34.67
                     Telefax: (21) 573.34.67

IRELAND – IRLANDE
Government Supplies Agency
Publications Section
4/5 Harcourt Road
Dublin 2   Tel. 661.31.11
                Telefax: 475.27.60

ISRAEL – ISRAËL
Praedicta
5 Shatner Street
P.O. Box 34030
Jerusalem 91430   Tel. (2) 52.84.90/1/2
                       Telefax: (2) 52.84.93

R.O.Y. International
P.O. Box 13056
Tel Aviv 61130   Tel. (3) 546 1423
                      Telefax: (3) 546 1442

Palestinian Authority/Middle East:
INDEX Information Services
P.O.B. 19502
Jerusalem   Tel. (2) 27.12.19
                 Telefax: (2) 27.16.34

ITALY – ITALIE
Libreria Commissionaria Sansoni
Via Duca di Calabria 1/1
50125 Firenze   Tel. (055) 64.54.15
                     Telefax: (055) 64.12.57
Via Bartolini 29
20155 Milano   Tel. (02) 36.50.83

Editrice e Libreria Herder
Piazza Montecitorio 120
00186 Roma Tel. 679.46.28
Telefax: 678.47.51

Libreria Hoepli
Via Hoepli 5
20121 Milano Tel. (02) 86.54.46
Telefax: (02) 805.28.86

Libreria Scientifica
Dott. Lucio de Biasio 'Aeiou'
Via Coronelli, 6
20146 Milano Tel. (02) 48.95.45.52
Telefax: (02) 48.95.45.48

JAPAN – JAPON
OECD Publications and Information Centre
Landic Akasaka Building
2-3-4 Akasaka, Minato-ku
Tokyo 107 Tel. (81.3) 3586.2016
Telefax: (81.3) 3584.7929

KOREA – CORÉE
Kyobo Book Centre Co. Ltd.
P.O. Box 1658, Kwang Hwa Moon
Seoul Tel. 730.78.91
Telefax: 735.00.30

MALAYSIA – MALAISIE
University of Malaya Bookshop
University of Malaya
P.O. Box 1127, Jalan Pantai Baru
59700 Kuala Lumpur
Malaysia Tel. 756.5000/756.5425
Telefax: 756.3246

MEXICO – MEXIQUE
OECD Publications and Information Centre
Edificio INFOTEC
Av. San Fernando no. 37
Col. Toriello Guerra
Tlalpan C.P. 14050
Mexico D.F.
Tel. (525) 606 00 11 Extension 100
Fax : (525) 606 13 07

Revistas y Periodicos Internacionales S.A. de C.V.
Florencia 57 - 1004
Mexico, D.F. 06600 Tel. 207.81.00
Telefax: 208.39.79

NETHERLANDS – PAYS-BAS
SDU Uitgeverij Plantijnstraat
Externe Fondsen
Postbus 20014
2500 EA's-Gravenhage Tel. (070) 37.89.880
Voor bestellingen: Telefax: (070) 34.75.778

**NEW ZEALAND –
NOUVELLE-ZÉLANDE**
GPLegislation Services
P.O. Box 12418
Thorndon, Wellington Tel. (04) 496.5655
Telefax: (04) 496.5698

NORWAY – NORVÈGE
NIC INFO A/S
Bertrand Narvesens vei 2
P.O. Box 6512 Etterstad
0606 Oslo 6 Tel. (022) 57.33.00
Telefax: (022) 68.19.01

PAKISTAN
Mirza Book Agency
65 Shahrah Quaid-E-Azam
Lahore 54000 Tel. (42) 353.601
Telefax: (42) 231.730

PHILIPPINE – PHILIPPINES
International Booksource Center Inc.
Rm 179/920 Cityland 10 Condo Tower 2
HV dela Costa Ext cor Valero St.
Makati Metro Manila Tel. (632) 817 9676
Telefax : (632) 817 1741

POLAND – POLOGNE
Ars Polona
00-950 Warszawa
Krakowskie Przedmieácie 7 Tel. (22) 264760
Telefax : (22) 268673

PORTUGAL
Livraria Portugal
Rua do Carmo 70-74
Apart. 2681
1200 Lisboa Tel. (01) 347.49.82/5
Telefax: (01) 347.02.64

SINGAPORE – SINGAPOUR
Gower Asia Pacific Pte Ltd.
Golden Wheel Building
41, Kallang Pudding Road, No. 04-03
Singapore 1334 Tel. 741.5166
Telefax: 742.9356

SPAIN – ESPAGNE
Mundi-Prensa Libros S.A.
Castelló 37, Apartado 1223
Madrid 28001 Tel. (91) 431.33.99
Telefax: (91) 575.39.98

Mundi-Prensa Barcelona
Consell de Cent No. 391
08009 – Barcelona Tel. (93) 488.34.92
Telefax: (93) 487.76.59

Llibreria de la Generalitat
Palau Moja
Rambla dels Estudis, 118
08002 – Barcelona
(Subscripcions) Tel. (93) 318.80.12
(Publicacions) Tel. (93) 302.67.23
Telefax: (93) 412.18.54

SRI LANKA
Centre for Policy Research
c/o Colombo Agencies Ltd.
No. 300-304, Galle Road
Colombo 3 Tel. (1) 574240, 573551-2
Telefax: (1) 575394, 510711

SWEDEN – SUÈDE
CE Fritzes AB
S–106 47 Stockholm Tel. (08) 690.90.90
Telefax: (08) 20.50.21

Subscription Agency/Agence d'abonnements :
Wennergren-Williams Info AB
P.O. Box 1305
171 25 Solna Tel. (08) 705.97.50
Telefax: (08) 27.00.71

SWITZERLAND – SUISSE
Maditec S.A. (Books and Periodicals - Livres
et périodiques)
Chemin des Palettes 4
Case postale 266
1020 Renens VD 1 Tel. (021) 635.08.65
Telefax: (021) 635.07.80

Librairie Payot S.A.
4, place Pépinet
CP 3212
1002 Lausanne Tel. (021) 320.25.11
Telefax: (021) 320.25.14

Librairie Unilivres
6, rue de Candolle
1205 Genève Tel. (022) 320.26.23
Telefax: (022) 329.73.18

Subscription Agency/Agence d'abonnements :
Dynapresse Marketing S.A.
38 avenue Vibert
1227 Carouge Tel. (022) 308.07.89
Telefax: (022) 308.07.99

See also – Voir aussi :
OECD Publications and Information Centre
August-Bebel-Allee 6
D-53175 Bonn (Germany) Tel. (0228) 959.120
Telefax: (0228) 959.12.17

THAILAND – THAÏLANDE
Suksit Siam Co. Ltd.
113, 115 Fuang Nakhon Rd.
Opp. Wat Rajbopith
Bangkok 10200 Tel. (662) 225.9531/2
Telefax: (662) 222.5188

TUNISIA – TUNISIE
Grande Librairie Spécialisée
Fendri Ali
Avenue Haffouz Imm El-Intilaka
Bloc B 1 Sfax 3000 Tel. (216-4) 296 855
Telefax: (216-4) 298.270

TURKEY – TURQUIE
Kültür Yayinlari Is-Türk Ltd. Sti.
Atatürk Bulvari No. 191/Kat 13
Kavaklidere/Ankara
Tel. (312) 428.11.40 Ext. 2458
Telefax: (312) 417 24 90
Dolmabahce Cad. No. 29
Besiktas/Istanbul Tel. (212) 260 7188

UNITED KINGDOM – ROYAUME-UNI
HMSO
Gen. enquiries Tel. (171) 873 8242
Postal orders only:
P.O. Box 276, London SW8 5DT
Personal Callers HMSO Bookshop
49 High Holborn, London WC1V 6HB
Telefax: (171) 873 8416
Branches at: Belfast, Birmingham, Bristol,
Edinburgh, Manchester

UNITED STATES – ÉTATS-UNIS
OECD Publications and Information Center
2001 L Street N.W., Suite 650
Washington, D.C. 20036-4922 Tel. (202) 785.6323
Telefax: (202) 785.0350

Subscriptions to OECD periodicals may also be placed
through main subscription agencies.

Les abonnements aux publications périodiques de
l'OCDE peuvent être souscrits auprès des principales
agences d'abonnement.

Orders and inquiries from countries where Distributors
have not yet been appointed should be sent to: OECD
Publications Service, 2, rue André-Pascal, 75775 Paris
Cedex 16, France.

Les commandes provenant de pays où l'OCDE n'a pas
encore désigné de distributeur peuvent être adressées à :
OCDE, Service des Publications, 2, rue André-Pascal,
75775 Paris Cedex 16, France.

1-1996